Missioners

Alive Publishing Ltd

Missioners

priest and people today

by

Archbishop Vincent Nichols

First published in 2007 by Alive Publishing Ltd,
Graphic House, 124 City Road, Stoke on Trent ST4 2PH
Tel: +44 (0) 1782 745600 Fax: +44 (0) 1782 745500
e-mail:editor@biblealive.co.uk

© 2007 Vincent Nichols
British Library Catalogue-in-Publication Data. A catalogue
record for this book is available from the British Library.

ISBN 978-0-9540335-8-3

This book is dedicated to the priests and deacons
of the Archdiocese of Birmingham.

Contents

Introduction

It may well be a surprise to many, as it was to me, to learn that Catholic parishes in England, with which we are so familiar, were not formally established in Church law until 1918. This is well worth remembering at a time when patterns of Church life, in the Catholic community, are changing and some of the assumptions of the last one hundred years are being challenged. Every Catholic church may no longer be at the heart of its own canonical parish; every parish may not have its own residential parish priest. Parishes may now be exploring ways of cooperating together rather than striving for autonomy; they may well be sharing resources rather than protecting them for exclusive advantage.

In this endeavour there is much to be learned from our history, particularly since the eighteenth century. At that time the role of the clergy gradually increased in Catholic life, not least with the fading of private chaplaincies, the growth of priestly formation in England, the restoration of the hierarchy and, of course, rapid industrialisation. Slowly, parish life emerged from the more scattered missions, sometimes called 'riding missions'. The role of the priest centred more round a constant and reliable provision of sacramental life and the authority that goes with it. Increasingly, too, administrative responsibility fell on the shoulders of the priest as the structures and property of the church grew apace.

Parochial life emerged slowly. It came with the appointment of priests by the bishop as 'missionary rectors'. They were still imbued with the sense of working in a difficult and at times hostile environment, yet became established with all the duties and rights which go with the task and status of 'rector'.

Throughout this history, and still powerfully evident today, certain themes and characteristics of the priests' life and ministry remain constant: the nature of his ordination; the dedication to Christ required of him; the bond of trust that exists between a priest and his people; the love and esteem in which a faithful priest is held; the essential importance of cooperation between priest and people in the work of the Church. These do not change essentially, although emphases come and go, and occasionally crises have to be lived through.

The chapters of this book reflect on these enduring themes. They do so not from a historical point of view, but more in a contemporary manner. They are drawn from homilies given in the last five years at the ordinations of priests and deacons. However, these brief historical reflections do help to set the scene.

We can be reassured that the challenges faced today by us all in the changing patterns of priestly ministry are not taking us into entirely uncharted waters. Experience and inspiration are to be found throughout our own history, and it is important that we become aware of it.

I am particularly grateful to Judith Champ for the many ways in which she makes that history available. The most outstanding contribution she has made, thus far, is her new biography of Bishop Ullathorne, Bishop of Birmingham from 1846-1888. Entitled *William Bernard Ullathorne: A Different Kind of Monk* it is a treasury of encouragement for all who have the good of the Church at heart today and who work for that good. It is certainly a great encouragement to me personally and, I am sure, to many priests who follow in the footsteps of those who worked with Bishop Ullathorne.

If there is one particular perspective I would draw from all that he did and wrote it is his emphasis on how he saw his diocesan priests. He was a Benedictine, yet over the years of his episcopal ministry he developed a real sense of the difficulties and rewards of diocesan priesthood.

His concerns, and his appreciation, centred round two phrases.

In the first place he disliked the phrase the 'secular clergy'. Of course he understood that the word 'denoted not their spirit but the field of their labours'[1]. Yet he feared that the use of the phrase 'is like giving a dog a bad name even though it be consecrated by long usage and incorporated into law' [2]. He feared the phrase 'secular' might be taken to indicate that diocesan clergy were less religious or less dedicated than the men of the religious orders and that they lived a more secular, and less worthy, way of life.

In this he was not entirely wrong, for in the mind of the people this can indeed occur. I recall well, as a young priest in St Anne's, Overbury Street, Liverpool, being told by some parishioners, somewhat self-righteously, that they had stopped going to St Anne's when 'the real priests' – the Benedictines – had left. It is also true that the same lack of self-esteem can enter at times into the mind of a diocesan priest himself.

Bishop Ullathorne much preferred the title 'Pastoral Priest' as the one fitting the diocesan priesthood. He held that the Lord's words 'You do not belong to the world because my choice withdrew you from the world' (John 15:19) applied to all priests alike and he knew that the diocesan priests had to be 'well-springs of light and grace' and 'authoritative witnesses' in the world to God's brightness and purity. The pastoral work of the diocesan priest was his defining character, as all would accept today. Ullathorne was unambiguous in wanting that to be made plain in the terminology used to describe the priest.

It is, of course, this pastoral character of the priest, his constant care for his people combined particularly with his sacramental ministry, which gives rise to the use of the term 'Father' as the best loved title of a priest today.

The second phrase, or word, which highlights Bishop Ullathorne's understanding of this pastoral priesthood is the word 'missioner'. He saw the priesthood in his own time and situation as essentially missionary. He expected his priests to take the same view and to have the same inspiration.

In 1853, at a Diocesan Synod, he made this heartfelt appeal:

> *'We are missioners! O name, rich with the most noble and generous associations! Our work is that of the apostles... Unless he make himself into a sacrifice, as an apostle would, for the souls of his brethren, he may be a priest, but he is unworthy to call himself a missioner. A missioner is a priest, laborious, patient, not easily discouraged, ingenious by that force of ardour which the spirit of his position enkindles to meet wants as they arise.'* [3]

Now these are words that have a real contemporary ring to them. They do not suggest a moving away from the stability of parish life, from pastoral ministry into some 'free-floating' and, often, over-individualistic particular ministry. They have nothing to do with the false dichotomy which has been put forward between 'maintenance and mission', for no one could have been more concerned with the establishment, good order and maintenance of the Church's life and

institutions than Bishop Ullathorne. Rather his insistence
was on the inner spirit and intention of the life and work of
the priest, and through him of the entire community. And this
is true for us today.

Bishop Ullathorne did not want priests who saw
themselves as 'settled freeholders'[4] content with what they
had and striving solely to hold onto it. Nor did he want
parish communities to have that attitude either. So, too,
today a priest who sees his task as simply that of celebrating
sacraments at the set times and keeping the administration
ticking over, even if he has more than one parish to care for,
is not on the right lines. Rather, to live up to both his heritage
and his calling, a priest needs the spirit that Ullathorne rightly
called that of a missioner. If he has the desire to lead people
in their journey to God, then this will be the desire and
achievement of the people too, not simply for themselves but
for all with whom they come into contact.

Ullathorne's vision of pastoral priests inspired by a
missionary enthusiasm fits our needs today. Such priests,
and there are many of them, fulfil their ministry in the midst
of a Catholic community showing the same characteristics.
Such a community will be ready and generous with its
pastoral compassion for those in need. (Last year the parishes
of the Archdiocese of Birmingham gave over £750,000 to
CAFOD alone, apart from many, many other charities both
local and overseas). Such a community will work hard on

passing on faith to its children and sharing faith in adult ventures. Here the sick will be visited and cared for, and the bereaved will receive sensitive and lasting support. The dead will be buried in great faith and mutual consolation.

A parish with a missionary spirit will reach out to those nearby with the invitation of faith, in the promise of prayer for those in need, with words and actions of encouragement and practical help. Most importantly, a missionary parish will know that its sole source of unity and strength is Christ himself, who shares his mission with them through the sacraments. The careful and reverent celebration of Mass will be at the heart of this community, for it is in Christ's sacrifice alone that his mission is fulfilled and the parish's begins.

In presenting his vision of the pastoral priest, Bishop Ullathorne was very aware that diocesan clergy, unlike religious priests, did not have a 'rule of life' or, as he put it, 'a system drawn out and constantly kept before them as to a perfection belonging to their state at which they should aim.'[5] The provision of such a vision, and such a document, is something beyond the scope of this small book. Yet, perhaps, some of the elements might be found here, for these chapters present what seem to me to be the enduring foundations, inspirations and expressions of the life of the pastoral priest, today's missioner.

Many of the priests of the Archdiocese of Birmingham have heard these themes in the homilies in which they were first expressed. I would like to dedicate this work to them, for theirs is a fine presbyterate, one of which Bishop Ullathorne would be proud, but also, at times, not uncritical. So many strive to live by the qualities he outlined, showing great patience, not easily discouraged and ingenious in finding ways of meeting the new and varied demands of each day.

I thank them sincerely.

✠ Vincent Nichols
Archbishop of Birmingham

Notes

[1] Discourse to the Clergy, Diocesan Synod 1864,
   William Bernard Ullathorne, Champ, Judith p395

[2] Ullathorne to Grant, 19 August 1868, Ibid., p395

[3] Ibid., p394

[4] Ibid., p394

[5] Ibid., p395

Missioners

From St Paul's Second Letter to the Corinthians

Unlike other people, we need no letters of recommendation either to you or from you, because you are yourselves our letter, written in our hearts that anyone can see and read, and it is plain that you are a letter from Christ, drawn up by us and written not with ink but with the Spirit of the living God, not on stone tablets but on the tablets of your living hearts.

Before God we are confident of this through Christ: not that we are qualified in ourselves to claim anything as our own work: all our qualifications come from God. He is the one who has given us the qualifications to be administrators of this new covenant, which is not a covenant of written letters but of the Spirit: the written letters bring death, but the Spirit gives life. Now if the administering of death, in the written letters engraved on stones, was accompanied by such a brightness that the Israelites could not bear looking at the face of Moses, though it was a brightness that faded, then how much greater will be the brightness that surrounds the administering of the Spirit! For if there was any splendour in administering condemnation, there must be very much greater splendour in administering justification. In fact, compared with this greater splendour, the thing that used to have such splendour now seems to have none; and if what was so temporary had any splendour, there must be much more in what is going to last for ever.

Having this hope, we can be quite confident; not like Moses, who put a veil over his face so that the Israelites would not notice the ending of what had to fade. And anyway, their minds had been dulled; indeed, to this very day, that same veil is still there when the old covenant is being read, a veil never lifted, since Christ alone can remove it. Yes, even today, whenever Moses is read, the veil is over their minds. It will not be removed until they turn to the Lord. Now this Lord is the Spirit, and where the Spirit of the Lord is, there is freedom. And we, with our unveiled faces reflecting like mirrors the brightness of the Lord, all grow brighter and brighter as we are turned into the image that we reflect; this is the work of the Lord who is Spirit.

Chapter 3:2-18

Earthenware Jars

Based on the homily given at the Ordination to the Priesthood
of Robert Murphy, St Chad's Cathedral, 21 July 2001

The ordination of a priest is always a wonderful occasion. It marks the culmination of many years preparation and the fulfilment of the hopes of both the new priest and his family. As a family gathers for an ordination these days, those hopes may well be ambiguous. Quite often the length of preparation has seemed inexplicably protracted, when quicker results are expected in other walks of life. Often hopes are mingled with anxieties in the awareness that the life of the priest is far from easy. Yet, overall, a family comes to appreciate the deep desire for priesthood that has taken root in the soul of this young man and is happy to support him in that desire and to see it fulfilled.

Indeed the family will sense that great things lie in store. The life of a priest holds out what can seem to be a limitless adventure. The priest will go where he is sent, off into an unknown, even if it is within the confines of the diocese. There he will meet an almost endless procession of people with whom he will have a quite unique relationship. He will be welcomed into their lives and trusted with confidences. He will be a witness to their sorrows and joys, as well as keeping company with them in the tedious times of life. He will celebrate with them the feasts of the year and with them observe its fasts. And he will do all this in order to serve their faith and their journey to salvation.

All this takes its definitive shape on the day of priestly ordination when, in the words of St Paul, the priest receives from God 'the qualifications to be the administrators of this new covenant' (2 Corinthians 3:6). And, as St Paul adds, 'this administration is surrounded with brightness and splendour'(v.9-10).

Indeed, in this passage St Paul unfolds the joy and expectation that fill our hearts on an ordination day. He tells us that this work of administration is the work of the Holy Spirit, who alone gives life. During this ceremony, in words, song and action, we invoke the Holy Spirit to fill the new priest with his gifts, to clothe him in holiness, to bind him utterly to the Lord, and to allow the brightness of this new covenant to shine from within him.

'Now this Lord is the Spirit, and where the Spirit of the Lord is, there is freedom. And we, with unveiled faces reflecting like mirrors the brightness of the Lord, all grow brighter and brighter as we are turned into the image that we reflect; this is the work of the Lord who is Spirit.'
(2 Corinthians 3:16-18)

There are indeed many bright faces here today!

It is rather obvious to state that St Paul is a true model and patron for a new priest. But it is a thought I would like to follow for a few moments.

In the first place, Paul was a fearless preacher. And preaching is a priority for every priest today. He is to be a herald of the Gospel, striving to find the words, the images, the right intensity of thought and emotion to get across to his listeners. This is no easy task for we are all saturated with communication, constantly presented with news, views, appeals, information and advice. So what can we learn from St Paul?

There are three qualities displayed by him for which we must strive.

In the first place, as a preacher, Paul was intellectually robust. His arguments were clear; his logic at times ruthless. He knew what he was up against and he tried to tackle issues head on.

One example of this is to be found in the passage I've already quoted. In it he is arguing for the effectiveness of the new covenant in comparison with that of the old. The comparisons he draws are bold and unambiguous. The old order was based on what was written down, whether in books or 'on stone tablets'. Yet this dispensation did not deliver life but only frustration and minds that were dulled. Nevertheless, the old order was accompanied by such brightness 'that the Israelites could not bear looking at the face of Moses'. (v.7)

Paul does not hesitate to point out that this brightness was destined to fade, for it was preparatory of a new and greater covenant. This cannot be understood by those wedded to that old covenant, whose minds remain 'veiled'. Indeed, 'Christ alone can remove it'. (v.15) All must turn to the Lord.

Quite logically, as the administrator of this new covenant, Paul will have nothing to do with the written word. The followers of Christ are not 'people of the book'. He will not rely on letters of testimony. Rather he holds up as his guarantor the evidence of the work of the Holy Spirit among the people.

'You are yourselves our letter, written in our hearts, that anyone can see and read and it is plain that you are a letter from Christ, drawn up by us and written not with ink but with the Spirit of the living God, not on stone tablets but on the tablets of your living hearts.' (2 Corinthians 3:2-4)

His argument is clear. No one could be in any doubt as to where his trust lay. It is not in a book or a text. It is in a person whom he knows and loves as his Lord. He has indeed broken free from the limited perspectives of his upbringing and found a new and exhilarating freedom in Christ. His words are powerful and convincing.

In tackling some of the issues of today, we can only strive to imitate St Paul. Whenever we seek to develop a theme in our preaching, whether it is doctrinal or a spiritual application of a saving truth, then we must seek out its underlying logic and make it as clear as we can.

Occasionally I receive complaints about the preaching offered to parishioners today. Mostly the complaints are about the lack of depth in what is said. 'We are not really being fed' is a phrase that is repeated. Preparation, reading, prayerful reflection: these alone can give rise to thoughtful, robust homilies which nurture, and challenge, our faith.

A second characteristic of the preaching of St Paul is that he was culturally sensitive. He paid attention to the circumstances, the background, the attitude of mind of his hearers. He was not one for ready-made sermons taken off the shelf or from the files of a computer. Each time and place has its own background agenda which could be used to his advantage.

When in Rome he was intensely aware of the Roman creation of a legal system and a good order that flowed from it. Indeed he was in Rome precisely in order to appeal to that law. Not surprisingly, then, an underlying theme of his preaching to the Romans takes the image of the law and shows how Christ entirely transforms it. He does not denigrate the law, recognising its civilising role, especially with regard to our sinfulness. But he claims that incorporation into Christ takes us beyond the realm of the law. Here is an entirely new remedy for sin, the Law of God, the rule of grace, made visible and accessible in Christ Jesus.

When speaking with the Corinthians with their Greek background and culture, a central theme he employed was wisdom. Wisdom was a gift, a gift of the gods, to which Greek culture aspired. In writing to the Corinthians, Paul uses it to open up the gift of God in Christ, describing him as 'the power of God and the wisdom of God' (1 Corinthians 1:25) relating the claims of the Gospel to the hopes and often unspoken desires of his audience.

Paul also tried to utilise a similar kind of cultural sensitivity when addressing the people of Athens at the Council of the Areopagus. His opening words are well known: 'I have seen for myself how extremely scrupulous you are in all religious matters ...' (Acts 17:22). It is also well known that his approach did not succeed on that occasion, but it remains a good example to us, nevertheless.

What would we focus on today if we were to begin our preparation for a homily with the same words? What preoccupies people today? What do we notice as the underlying context or framework of thought and action in modern Britain?

Perhaps we would pay more attention to all the ramifications of the 'globalisation' that actually shape our modern way of life. Events from all over the world impact on our lives. Global economics dictate the food we eat.

National identity is shaken in a shrinking world. To whom do we belong? Who are we now? Where does our identity come from? These are preoccupying undercurrents. The attentive preacher will use them. They may well be his way into a presentation of the universal truth of Christ and the truly 'catholic' nature of the Church.

Similarly the air we breathe is saturated with the deep individualism of modern culture, giving rise to an accompanying sense of isolation and fragmentation. These influences, in time, raise the entire project of 'social cohesion' which has such a powerful influence on government policy today. How do we hold together as a society? From where come the social norms of acceptable behaviour? It is not difficult to imagine Paul saying: 'I have seen for myself how extremely scrupulous you are in wanting to make sure that no one feels left out' and going on to expound the foundations and demands of our common life in Christ.

The third aspect of Paul's preaching that deserves our imitation is the spiritual depth he sustains in his writings. Constantly he addresses the quest of the disciple of Christ to be more closely united to him and to sustain the struggle against temptation and sin of every sort. Paul, like every true herald of the Gospel, is an expert in the human heart. He knows our tendencies to defeatism, to self-deceit, to arrogance, to self-centredness. He names what we know of ourselves and shows us how the grace of Christ can slowly draw us beyond ourselves into new life.

Paul explores this relationship between grace and nature as the drama of our pilgrimage of life. At times his language is powerful, emotive and evocative (Romans 7:24); at times it is lyrical (1 Corinthians 13:4-13); at times more measured and pragmatic (Romans 12:3-13). But at all times he is encouraging his hearers to be steadfastly honest about themselves and entirely open to Christ.

From the depth of Paul's own spiritual journey come these spiritual qualities that are so appealing and needed today. He has a dogged determination and a willingness to persevere that is second to none. Quite simply, he is not going to be put off. He lists for us the obstacles he has overcome or endured: imprisonment and the lash, stoning and shipwrecks; danger from brigands, pagans and 'from my own people' (2 Corinthians 11:26); lack of sleep, hunger and thirst, cold and the lack of clothes. Then he adds his 'daily preoccupation: my anxiety for the churches. When anyone has had scruples, I have had scruples with him; when anyone is made to fall, I am tortured.' (2 Corinthians 1:28)

In the course of his life every priest is able to assemble his own list of his woes. I hope we do so as reluctantly as Paul and that our lists will be far less dramatic than his. But every good priest will share St Paul's last burden: 'anxiety for the churches', for the heart of a priest is one with the good of his people.

In imitating Paul the preacher today can have one overriding prayer: that, like him, we will be able to say at the end, 'I have fought the good fight to the end; I have run the race to the finish; I have kept the faith.' (2 Timothy 4:7)

If we are to succeed in making Paul's words our own, then there is one Pauline image that we need to keep always in view. In a way it sums up Paul's spiritual journey. It reveals the fundamental disposition of his heart. It is a stance that is fitting to all of us, and particularly to us priests.

'We are only the earthenware jars that hold this treasure to make it clear that such an overwhelming power comes from God and not from us.' (2 Corinthians 4:7)

In this image lies an important key to our ministry. This attitude of mind and heart is so important at this very moment when the new priest receives this 'overwhelming power'. In this ceremony he is given the power of consecration and the power of absolution. To change bread and wine into the Body and Blood of Christ is indeed an astonishing power. So too is the power to forgive sins in Christ's name. Yet we remain earthenware jars, today and always.

The image of earthenware fits very easily in a diocese which includes the Potteries. The skill of the potter, the designer, the artist, is found in abundance today, especially in the towns of Stoke-on-Trent, carried in the genetic pool of some communities. So many will be able to develop for themselves the image given by St Paul.

Earthenware vessels come in all shapes and sizes. So do we priests. There is no single model, no one mould from which we are all drawn. This, I believe, is a great encouragement to anyone who senses within himself the call of God to the priesthood. The Lord wants us as we are, so that He may shape us to be his finished work.

The analogy can be taken further. Some earthenware is tough and oven-ready; other pieces are clearly for more careful use; some are esteemed for their design and beauty which both reflects and creates an environment of refinement and finesse. Priests, too, have different talents and strengths which need to be appreciated. But we must not overplay the analogy. The affection in which we hold each other is not ultimately related to an outward form but much more to a treasuring of the real and varied gifts which that outward form contains.

But beyond this rich variety, there are some qualities to be found in every priest and disciple of the Lord, qualities well contained within this analogy of 'earthenware vessels'. They are qualities for which every wise priest strives. They are, therefore, important to recall on the day of an ordination.

The first is the prime purpose of St Paul's analogy: we are merely the instruments of God's work and never its true author. Paul drives home this dimension of his analogy in forceful terms. He highlights the difficulties he faces, the persecution he suffers, the blows he endures. He spells out the feebleness of his own efforts so as 'to make it clear that such an overwhelming power comes from God.' (v.7)

A newly ordained priest is rightly feted. Many will rejoice in him, bringing him gifts and good wishes. He will be welcomed wherever he goes. But this must not go to his head, as it easily can. People certainly rejoice in the generosity of the gift of self the new priest has made, but they rejoice more in the prospect of God using him for fruitful ministry in the Church. High esteem for the office of priest must be matched by the humility in the heart of the priest, for humility is the virtue that puts us at the disposition of God rather than the pursuit of our own needs and ideas.

A good priest never falls into the trap of pride or exaggerated self-esteem. He remains aware of the 'instrumentality' of his ministry. As it is well put: I am no more than a biro in the Lord's hand, to be picked up or left unused as he wishes.

The second application of this analogy to the life of the priest gives us a reminder of our fragility. 'Earthenware jars' are easily chipped, cracked or broken. No matter their provenance or purpose, crockery is essentially fragile and needs appropriately careful handling.

Now the first responsibility for the way we are treated lies with ourselves. We have a substantial duty to take care of ourselves, our physical and spiritual wellbeing. Ordination does not create 'supermen'. Our fragility remains. Every priest needs to ensure that he does not allow his heart, his thoughts, his imaginings, or his actions to chip away at the flaws and cracks of his nature. If that happens the cracks grow wider until the priest is in real trouble. Under pressure the cracks give way and the vessel lies broken. Through attentiveness and care, on the other hand, priests do well to keep an eye on each other, bringing to each other that particular sensitivity to the stresses of their ministry. Good friends also do the same, not being afraid to remind the priest of his vulnerability and of the need to take care. We must take care of each other.

The third aspect of the image of the priest as 'earthenware jars' is equally important. In fact, the earthenware jar of our self is constantly being refashioned. In many ways, we remain clay in the hands of the potter. He shapes and reshapes us so that we can be fit for purpose in each situation in which we minister his grace.

The day of ordination is, of course, a point of great arrival. A long process of formation is complete. But it is true to say that today an even longer process of formation is beginning. I am no longer the priest I was on the day of my ordination. So many events, circumstances and, most of all, people have shaped and reshaped this earthenware vessel. This is the course of ministry. Every priest is called, day by day, to be responsive to so many situations. Some he will deal with readily and competently. Others will be beyond him, taking him to breaking point. They will drive him back to the Lord in prayer. Then he is back in the skilful hands of the master potter.

Occasionally we can experience real trauma and breakdown. Then we are back on the potter's wheel, having lost our previous coherence, waiting to be remoulded in a manner which he alone knows and is able to achieve.

At moments such as these, which come in the life of every priest, the first and most important point of St Paul's analogy remains of paramount importance. It is always the treasure that matters, not the vessel. If at times the world sees only broken vessels – and sometimes shouts this aloud – the eyes of faith always strive to see the treasure they still contain. And God never withdraws that treasure even when the jar is leaking, badly cracked or, finally, fallen to pieces. The treasure is always there, waiting for us to put ourselves into his hands so that he can reshape us to be filled again with his love, his graciousness, his brightness.

The life of a priest is indeed a great adventure. It is not the steady, well-planned route of a professional career moving towards retirement and leisure. It starts with a total gift of self in response to the glimpsing of a treasure. And seeking after the Lord remains its secret heart.

Missioners

From the Prophet Jeremiah

Listen, nations, to the word of Yahweh.
Tell this to the distant islands,
'He who scattered Israel gathers him,
he guards him as a shepherd guards his flock.'
For Yahweh has ransomed Jacob, rescued him from a hand
stronger than his own.
They will come and shout for joy on the heights of Zion,
they will throng towards the good things of Yahweh:
corn and oil and wine,
sheep and oxen;
Their soul will be like a watered garden, they will sorrow no more.
The virgin will then take pleasure in the dance,
young men and old will be happy;
I will change their mourning into gladness,
comfort them, give them joy after their troubles,
refresh my priests with rich food,
and see my people have their fill of my good things
- it is Yahweh who speaks.

Jeremiah 31:10-14

The Pastor of his People

Based on the homily given at the Ordination to the Priesthood
of Paul Edwards, Holy Trinity Church, Sutton Coldfield,
21 November 2001

The 'pastoral priest' was the description of the clergy preferred by Bishop William Ullathorne in his addresses to them in the 1860s. He disliked the term 'secular priesthood' because it seemed to place the priest too close to the ways and habits of the world.

Indeed this is always a danger for every priest, and bishop! The temptations to 'go with the flow' are considerable and like all temptations, they hold out something which is attractive and which would appear to advance our cause. A familiarity with the ways of the age is surely essential to an effective preaching of the Gospel. So, too, is an appreciation of the pressures and tensions under which people live. To be excused these places a priest in an artificial world and can lead him into an indifference about the pressures, expectations and sheer weight of opinion to which most people are subjected. If, as priests, we do indeed enjoy a degree of security unfamiliar to most of our people we must be very careful as to how we use that privilege.

Such a privilege is surely not for our comfort. Certainly people do not begrudge us a degree of wellbeing but only so that we are able to fulfil our calling and the high expectations they have of us. It is this generosity, and high expectations, that make recent scandals so hurtful to the Catholic community. As has often been said, one of the most destructive strands of the abuse of children within the Church is the betrayal of trust that it involves. That is true, of course, of all forms of abuse, but the abuse of a child by a priest attacks the root of a trust given in faith, and therefore attacks that faith itself. Indeed, victims of abuse constantly testify that not only has their ability to trust, and love, been severely damaged but also their capacity for faith and prayer itself. Over this there is much for us to repent.

The support and privilege given to us priests, on the other hand, is provided for two interlocking purposes. The first is that, as priests, we have time to pray, to reflect, to read; in a phrase, to be close to God. The second is that we have the freedom to be present among and for our people, so that we can meet their proper spiritual and pastoral needs. These two are obviously inter-related. The quality of a priest's presence, his readiness for Mass, for visiting the dying, for encouraging the young, will depend entirely on the depth of his own spiritual life.

In accepting the support given by the people, then, every priest is entering into a contract with them. By that implicit contract he agrees to be their priest, their pastor, and so become an important part of their lives. He is to know their world, their hopes and fears. He is to feel the same chill winds that they do. He shares in their joys and sorrows, their anxieties and dreads. But he does so in a unique way, not as a neighbour, nor as a relative, not as a healthcare professional, nor as any other professional. He is not a manager of the lives of others, nor a therapist. No, he is their priest, their pastor, their spiritual father.

To fulfil that role, which is so difficult to tie down, requires great pastoral skill. It is, in a way, a rare skill. Not only is it needed in the priest but it must also be accepted by the people. And sometimes both the skill and the acceptance are lacking. Then parish life becomes formalised and much of its potential remains sadly unfulfilled.

So what can be said about the pastoral skill of the priest in his parish ministry? Of what does it consist? How does a priest go about acquiring such sensitivities and ability?

There are no simple answers to these questions. But there are some indications, I believe, and the reflections of this chapter may point to them. There are, indeed, ways in which a priest is entirely 'for this world', the world of his parish, while at the same time not totally 'of this world'. But what is certain is this: such a skill, such a manner of being present, is learned neither quickly nor in theory. It comes with time, with practice, and almost certainly, with mistakes and the pain they cause.

The good pastoral sense of a priest, being present for his people, seems to me to have six dimensions. Together they make up the skill of true pastoral care. Together they tell us why the outstanding pastors of the Church are declared to be saints. They also make clear why most of us priests simply struggle to do the best we can.

First, a pastoral priest has a strong sense of place. He knows his parish, his patch.

One of the joys I have found in being a bishop is spending time with a priest in his parish. Sometimes, but not often enough, I can go out to visit the sick, accompanied by the priest. Often he will give me a running commentary on the streets we are walking: who lives there; what happened here; what sadness lies behind those doors; what plans are being formed for this or that new development. He reminds me of a gardener showing visitors around his garden, telling them about the quality of the soil here, the advantages of this shady spot, the dangers of high winds in that corner, pointing out both his successes and disasters. I imagine a vineyard keeper might do the same. Here is the priest walking through that part of the vineyard entrusted to him by the Lord, knowledgeable of its fertility and its dangers, aware of all that shapes and threatens its fruitfulness.

To use a different language, the pastoral priest will be something of an expert in the particular culture of his parish. He will know its idiom and preoccupation, the history of failure or disaster that still casts its shadows. He will know how best to speak to his people, to interpret events and to

present the message of the Gospel and the teaching of the
Church in a way that is pertinent and instructive.

If a priest is to acquire this true pastoral sense of place then
there are certain temptations he will have to overcome.

In the first place he will have to move beyond the
restlessness that he may feel, the desire simply to be
elsewhere. Of course this is a temptation that affects
everyone at some time or another. But it can play a
significant part in the life of a priest.

How easy it is to think, quite simply, that other parishes
are better. As priests we can quickly succumb to the idea that
the problems we struggle with here would be lifted from our
shoulders if only we could move elsewhere. Other parishes,
of course, don't have problems! And how difficult it is when
the people of a parish begin to sense that this idea has taken
root in the soul of their priest. The valiant pray for him more
than ever, for a discontented priest is a burden for all. The
less valiant barricade their hearts and spirit to the unspoken
messages of their priest and struggle on in their pilgrimage.
Others just turn away.

The wise priest, who is growing in pastoral skill, refrains
from such comparisons. Nor does he retreat into a dulling
attitude of mind that says all parishes are equally difficult so
'what difference does it make anyway?'.

Rather he seeks to cultivate a simple yet profound sense
that God is here, in this place, with all its changes of fortune.

He knows that this is the place in which he has been placed, by God's providence. Here he will serve his Lord.

The late Pope John Paul II became well known for his habit of kissing the ground whenever he arrived in a new country. The origins of this gesture lay in his early life, as told by one of his biographers, quoting the young Karol Wojtyla himself:

> *'Karol began his ministry (in his first parish) with a symbolic gesture one day to become universally known: "It was harvest time," he recalled. "I walked through the fields of grain with the crops partly already reaped, and partly still waving in the wind. When I finally reached the territory of the Niegowic parish, I knelt down and kissed the ground. It was a gesture I had learned from St John Vianney."* [1]

A priest's pastoral skill will develop when he grows in these virtues of reverence for the place where he is, of stability of heart and perseverance. When he can say of his parish, 'This is a blessed place', while also recognising that it is marred, then he is indeed acquiring a missioner's spirit.

The second sense a pastoral priest acquires is a great sensitivity to his people.

This 'sense of the people' is, of course, closely connected to the priest's 'sense of place'. It is made up of all the awareness and knowledge of his people that is a pastoral priest's first stock-in-trade. It is shown in his endless talk of the people of his parish, their connections, the links between their families. It is often well displayed when a priest stands at the door of the church either before or after Mass with a word for everyone as they come and go.

Such knowledge, and the kindness that goes with it, is only acquired slowly. It comes with time spent in the classroom, at the school gate, with time given to visiting the homes of parishioners, either as a matter of routine or in conjunction with sacramental preparation. The old axiom remains true: a priest who doesn't visit his people doesn't know his parish.

Tributes paid to a priest often highlight the importance of this pastoral care. A couple rarely forget the priest who married them, nor parents the priest who baptised their children. The conduct of a funeral has a major impact on grieving relatives just as care for sick relatives is never forgotten. These are the actions which bind a priest to his people, the actions by which he becomes their 'Father'.

Yet this 'sense of the people' is also important in another way. An important part of the priest's task is to be maintainer of the unity of the parish. So the priest, above all others, needs an awareness of the factions and divisions within the community. He may not be able to resolve them. Nor should he become part of them. Rather, with this pastoral good sense he will know how to manage these divisions, keeping boundaries when necessary and tackling excesses when they occur.

This cumulative 'sense of the people' is often a real challenge today, especially in larger urban parishes. Unlike even just a few decades ago, the movement of people within a parish is remarkable. New faces will appear week by week, and stalwart families move on. So the challenge is to find ways of being aware of and welcoming the newcomers and ensuring that, no matter their nationality or culture, they feel 'at home' in a thoroughly Catholic sense. In such circumstances, this 'sense of the people' is a more demanding task today and one in which the priest and his key helpers will have to work together generously.

There are signs which indicate when this truly pastoral 'sense of the people' has not yet been acquired, or is seriously on the wane. A priest who constantly talks of his people as 'them' is hardly rich in this pastoral sensitivity. Nor is one who belittles his people, with constant reference to their weaknesses. But most pastoral priests resist these temptations, succumbing perhaps only through tiredness or frustration.

The growth of the compassion and solidarity which lie at the heart of this sensitivity springs from a closeness to the Lord. Only in him do we begin to see accurately and truly. Only with his eyes do we see his presence in every parishioner, knowing within our daily practice that these are indeed 'the holy people of God'.[2] Each day we priests can ask for a renewal of that grace, first indicated in our ordination ceremony. Only in this perspective will we foster the roots of the 'communion' of life in Christ that binds together all our people, and we to them, in the life of the Church.

The third 'sense' that contributes to the gracefulness of the pastoral priest is the grace of practical wisdom and, in particular, the 'sense of timing'.

The demands of the Gospel are, of course, constant. The pathway by which we are to come to the Lord, expressing fully in our lives the light and compassion of God, is clearly laid out. But we walk it only step by step, and not generally speaking, by leaps and bounds.

The sensitive pastor understands this. He knows how to accompany people on this journey of faith, knowing when to press, when to wait. He has good sense, practical wisdom, about what to ask for, when to act and when to refrain from acting.

Another way of expressing this is to say that the pastoral priest knows 'the seasons of the heart'. He knows when an individual, or a family, is entering an opportunity for a change of heart and a new start. Yet he also knows the seasons which are barren in that regard and the importance of his patience and stability during them.

Often crises provide key moments. The wise priest will know when to give priority time to those going through a crisis. He will also know those whose crisis has become habitual and could easily be intractably all-consuming. Part of this 'sense of timing' is knowing precisely when to withdraw or pass on to another, trained in clinical skills, those whose needs are beyond the skills of the priest. But the pastorally skilful priest will know when a person is ready to respond to a prompting of the Holy Spirit, even when that moment comes in experiences of pain or distress.

If this is true, and easily illustrated, in the pastoral care of an individual, then it is true also of a community, whether small and great. A chaplain to a school or hospital will likewise know the rhythms of its life and the periods in which his care is more needed than others. The death of a pupil is one such moment, when the message of Gospel hope suddenly finds a new openness in the heart of all in the school. Pastoral leadership for an entire local community is also sometimes required. One example lingers in my mind. On the day after the disaster in the Hillsborough football stadium involving so many Liverpool supporters, a service of Evening Prayer was quickly arranged in the Cathedral of Christ the King. It seemed as if the whole of Liverpool gathered in and around the Cathedral that night to be led in prayer by the city's two bishops. Official memorial services for those who tragically died were held much later. But that gathering was the fruit of a good pastoral sense of timing exercised at a city level. Its effect was remarkable.

The pastoral priest, then, knows how to wait, when to be patient and just 'to be'. He knows how to respond to key moments of grace, rather than to think it is always his duty to produce such moments and to drive them forward. He knows what is spoken of as 'the law of graduality', how we progress only step by step in our journey towards fulfilling the unchanging requirements of the Law of Love. The good priest resists the temptations of uniform diagnosis of pastoral situations and the uniform single solutions that are somehow meant to meet all needs. He will be blessed with practical wisdom, and that will bear much fruit in his ministry. In this he will be trusted.

A fourth 'sense' in the repertoire of the pastoral priest is focused on his sense of permanence and structure. As a pastoral priest he will care for the structures that give permanence to the community: the church, the parish hall, the school and the other institutions that are part of the enduring fabric of local life. No doubt this 'good sense' will at times be a burden, especially so in days of increasing bureaucracy and external supervision. But beyond these burdens, the priest will understand the importance of such structures in ensuring continuity, providing necessary comfort and 'shelter' in hard times and being focal points for the life of the community.

The good priest will resist the temptations to belittle or neglect the structures of his parish. Patterns of steady maintenance will be in place so that problems do not escalate to become crises. His will be a steady oversight and stewardship.

But he will also resist the temptation of making the buildings themselves into the focal point of his ministry. The constant change and improvement of property – often starting with the presbytery – is not the sign of a properly focused ministry. Property can easily become a preoccupation and a source of undue pride.

Rather, the pastoral priest will have a critical love and care for the institutions and buildings of his parish. His underlying aim is always that they serve the people, rather than vice versa. In all of this he will, wholeheartedly, enlist the help of the parishioners, instilling in them a proper sense of ownership and the scope of action that such responsibilities require. He will encourage parishioners to be school governors, not out of interest in their own children but for the good of all. He will look for architects, builders, plumbers, electricians, gardeners, cleaners and artists who will bring their skills and dedication to the service of the community. In this they will show their respect and esteem for their predecessors and make their own contribution to future generations.

Of all the structures and buildings of a parish the church, of course, is the most important. Here the family of God gathers to express its praise and to rejoice in the living presence of the Lord. That the church should be well cared for, clean and beautifully appointed goes without saying. Often such beauty is the most eloquent testimony to the abiding presence of God. And such beauty is, perhaps, the most powerful invitation to faith that we can offer today. Time spent in a beautiful church can be healing and uplifting in a way which goes beyond words. The work of ensuring such beauty is a primary work of evangelisation in our world today.

The last two 'senses' which the pastoral priest will develop and bring to his ministry relate in a special way to the heart of his ministry. As a man dedicated to serving the life of faith in his people, the priest will have his own well-rooted life of prayer. This will give rise in him to these two further dimensions: his 'sense of prayer' and his 'sense of the beyond'.

By a priest's 'sense of prayer' I mean not so much his own pattern of prayer and its importance as the skill with which he nurtures and fosters the life of prayer in his people. To me, this skill lies in one particular area today, which I want to explore briefly.

Part of our contemporary culture is to pay keen attention to experience, to our own experience and to that of others. Experience has been given a particular prominence, a particular credibility such that, for some, it has actually become the touchstone of 'truth'. They might say, 'Well it's true for me', as if that was all that mattered. So, too, the claim might be made that experience, understood essentially as emotions, is a most important component in the life of faith.

A discussion of these claims is not my purpose here. Rather, I simply want to assert the importance of moving from the realm of personal experience, whatever claims are made for it, into the wider realm of prayer. A sensitive priest can be a great leader in this process. Of course, others will do the same, but the priest, in particular, is well placed to help make this transition.

We begin this transition with the simple acknowledgement that our experiences are not the whole story. None of us is 'a world apart'; none of us is complete in ourselves. Nor is our human experience self-enclosed. No, we make sense of ourselves, as individuals and as humanity, only when we see our particular experiences, be they of overwhelming joy, weighty sorrow, broken heartedness or boredom, in the wider context of the faith. We have to bring our experiences before the Lord, holding them before him, looking at them again in this far wider context if we are to live those experiences in a wholesome way. Only when we place ourselves there can we find the sense of proportion and perspective that frees us from being absorbed in ourselves alone.

The leader in prayer, the good pastoral priest, knows how to assist in this process. He will help people not only to say their prayers but to bring themselves into those prayers. He, and other prayer guides, will open up the links between the experiences of the heart and the patterns of God's providence. Among other things he will know that at times of pain this is difficult to achieve. In those moments he will urge people to rely on their routine and favourite prayers.

A startling example of this for me came on a visit to the Dachau concentration camp in the suburbs of Munich. After visiting the exhibition and walking the length of the camp I was literally struck dumb with the horror of what had taken place there. I was so disturbed that when I entered the Catholic chapel at the far end of the site I found that I was totally and utterly unable to pray. At that moment I understood the insistence of some that silence is the only response to such a holocaust of evil. Yet as I sat silently in the church, ever so slowly the words of prayers were given to me. What came were words of the Psalms, though it could have been the Rosary.

And that is the role of the Church, the gift of the Spirit: to give us words when we have none; to take our experience and lift it into a higher context; to enable us to move from experience to prayer.

In times of great emotion we may well need the gentle skill of a prayer guide. Without any assistance we may simply remain within that emotion or even think that reflecting on it is itself prayer. There is a transition to be made: from experience to prayer. During that transition our awareness, our experience itself, will change: from grief to acceptance; from joy to praise; from darkness to resignation or hope; from anxiety to trustful petition. The wise priest knows how to help people make this change: he has a good 'sense of prayer' and of its power.

The church, of course, is a house of prayer. Everything in it should serve prayer. Everything that takes place should assist this transition. The church is not a place in which, essentially, we express or share our experiences. Rather we come to church to go beyond those experiences and transform them into prayer. Prayer is, after all, the raising of the mind and heart to God and not simply the expression of what fills our minds and hearts.

A First Holy Communion Mass, for example, is often inhibited by the strength of the families' excitement and joy. This, of course, is a special moment for them all, focused on their children. But the Mass is not a celebration of that joy. It is a prayer of praise to God who gives the gift of his presence in Christ in the Eucharist to these children for the first time. The challenge of moving from experience to prayer is the task facing every priest, and catechist, at that time.

So, too, a wedding ceremony does not centre on the experience of the couple nor on the feelings of the families, no matter how complex they might be. In one sense they can be left at the door of the church and picked up again at the wedding reception. These experiences belong in the church only as the starting point for the prayer of the wedding ceremony itself, the blessing it brings and the sacrament, the action of God, which is at its heart.

Helping people to make this transition from experience to prayer is so important. Yet it is not always easy for the priest who, day in and day out, carries out the rituals of prayer, often moving from children's Mass to funeral in a matter of hours. Sensitivity to the experience of those coming together to pray is crucial. But so too is the ability to go beyond that experience to the realm of prayer.

Just as experience needs prayer to find its salvation, so, too, prayer requires the experiences of the heart to find its dynamism. When the two become separated then each suffers seriously. For the priest, having to face at times a wide range of emotional experiences, cool detachment can seem the safest way forward. But his skill lies in knowing how to hold together the truth of the experiences of his people and the invitation of the Lord to lay it all at his feet in prayer.

The priest's daily celebration of Mass is the place to which he brings that full range of experiences – both his own and his people's – in order to unite them to Christ. What he holds in his heart will fill his prayers. Then his 'sense of prayer' will find its fulfilment.

The final pastoral sense which characterises a priest's ministry is, as already noted, a 'sense of the beyond'.

In its simplest form this sense is brought to a parish by a priest in the very act of his appointment. A priest is not chosen by the parish. He is sent. The priest, then, does not emerge from the parish's own sense of itself. He comes from without. Perhaps there will be an easy 'fit' between a priest and parish; perhaps not. But the very process itself is a healthy reminder that, as Catholics, the parish is part of a greater whole and never entire or closed in on itself.

This perspective has profound roots. The letter to St James points out strongly that the Gospel comes to us from without. We are never the authors of our own salvation, giving to ourselves that saving word. Rather it comes always as a gift and often in unexpected ways. In a minor way the arrival of a priest from the wider Church is a reminder of this truth: that we must always remain open to receiving the truth, never believing that we possess it.

The priest, in his person, represents the wider Church, and it is healthy when these links are developed. Awareness of neighbouring parishes, cooperation between them, attentiveness to the structure of the deanery and, in due measure, to the reality of the diocese are all features of true Catholic life which a priest embodies and knows how to foster. St Augustine spoke to his people in Hippo of the dangers of being self-contained. He warned them against being 'frogs in a pond', croaking away in self-importance, oblivious to the wider world. As Catholics it is, of course, from the wider world that we gain our identity.

The wise priest will ensure that these wider horizons are part of the life of his parish. He will ensure that concerns of justice, that action against poverty and need, are not confined to those nearby. Rather he will want his parish to be genuinely universal in its awareness and response. He will use the good offices of CAFOD and other agencies and institutions to put this into practice. His eye will always be on the wider horizon.

The widest of all horizons is, of course, that of eternity. A key to fruitful pastoral ministry is the way in which a priest keeps this horizon before the minds of his people.

I once sat with a priest who was struggling to fill in a diocesan pastoral return of one sort or another. One of the boxes he has to fill in concerned his current aims as parish priest. He was bemused. So I said, 'Father, what are you trying to achieve here?' 'To get people to heaven' he said! That was such a true answer and, fortuitously, it contains a bottom line that no one can inspect!!

But this is exactly the business of the priest. We may not tackle it today in the way of the past, with constant reminders of the eternal consequences of sin. But the good priest keeps this horizon well lit, not least in the witness of his own prayer and his own peacefulness.

Perhaps these six dimensions of the work of the pastoral priest help us to put together something of his 'rule of life'. The routines which fill a day can seem almost without pattern and consequence. Yet the pattern is there: the consistent, skilful exercise of pastoral care in these six ways. Together they make up the ministry of a priest, his own pathway to holiness. Together they form an attitude of mind, a daily dedication of heart, a 'rule of life' that expresses and shapes the calling of the 'secular priest'.

I return to that word 'secular', so disliked by Bishop Ullathorne. To him, in many ways, the world was a hostile place. Yet it is the proper realm of the priest's ministry. From the perspective of the pastoral priest, the secular world is a holy place, a place of God's unbounding grace. Today we appreciate this very much indeed.

Notes

[1] *Universal Father, A Life of Pope John Paul II* by Garry O'Connor, p122

[2] *Rite of Ordination,* (see p147)

Missioners

From the Book of Wisdom

O God of my fathers and Lord of mercy, who have made all things by your word, and by your wisdom have formed man to have dominion over the creatures you have made, and rule the world in holiness and righteousness, and pronounce judgement in uprightness of soul, give me the wisdom that sits by your throne, and do not reject me from among your servants. For I am your slave and the son of your maidservant, a man who is weak and short-lived, with little understanding of judgement and laws; for even if one is perfect among the sons of men, yet without the wisdom that comes from you, he will be regarded as nothing.

With you is wisdom, who knows your works and was present when you made the world, and who understands what is pleasing in your sight and what is right according to your commandments.

Send her forth from the holy heavens, and from the throne of your glory send her, that she may be with me and toil, and that I may learn what is pleasing to you, for she knows and understands all things, and she will guide me wisely in my actions and guard me with her glory.

Chapter 9:1-6, 9-10)

A Heart Wise and Shrewd

Based on the homily given at the Ordination to the Priesthood
of David Gnosill, St Peter's, Bloxwich, 26 July 2003

This ceremony of ordination to the priesthood is dramatic, in its gestures and words. But it is not a drama. It is elaborate in its movements and composition. But at heart it is simple. We human beings are the actors in this ceremony. But we are only instruments, for the ceremony is about something that we, of ourselves, could never achieve. This ceremony effects a radical change in the life of the candidate before us today. He becomes a priest. And only God can do that.

At the heart of this change lies the establishment of a new relationship. Ordination establishes a new bond between Christ and the new priest. The nature of that bond is important. This ceremony is not the signing of a new contract, a formal agreement, for the delivery of services. The basis of what is happening here is not to be properly understood through analogies with the caring professions. The priest is not so much one bound by a professional contract as one caught up and sealed in a relationship of love. That relationship is publicly proclaimed and effected today. And only God can do that.

For the priest, ordination establishes a new way of being. He is now bound to Christ as a priest in his innermost being, or 'ontologically' as we like to say. In one sense, this bond is not new. It has been deep inside the soul of the priest-to-be from the first moment of his existence, waiting for fulfilment. That fulfilment occurs today. Or at least it starts out today. For this reason the day of ordination is one of profound satisfaction. Something is indeed achieved: the fulfilling of a God given promise.

'Before I formed you in the womb I knew you; before you came to birth I consecrated you. I have appointed you as prophet to the nations.' (Jeremiah 1:5)

The candidate for priesthood has discovered this inner depth in himself. During his preparatory years he has sensed and explored this call, this destiny, and come to know it as the deepest truth of himself. His perception and conviction have been formed and tested by the Church, initially in the family and circle of faithful friends, and then within the seminary, the crucial community of formation. Today this journey comes to a defining moment. Today the new priest knows that he has indeed found his true self. He has found it in and through Jesus Christ the Priest. And we are witnesses to that.

The ceremony that takes place today is full of outward signs of this new inner reality.

Today we see the candidate prostrating himself on the floor of the church. Here is a gesture of total self-abandonment. All defences are down. Prostration is a posture of defencelessness and submission. That's why it is used in moments of capture and arrest. Yet here it is not forced. It is taken up willingly, out of love and in love. Here the gesture echoes the words of Mary: 'Let it be done to me, according to your will.' (Luke 1:38) and the words of Jesus to His Father: 'Let your will not mine be done.' (Luke 2:43) Today, as a new relationship with the Lord is being sealed, the new priest makes himself totally available to all that it will involve.

The consequences are seen almost immediately. The new priest's hands are anointed, an outward sign of the inner sealing of his heart. These hands are to be used to express the love of Christ which is now marking his soul.

The new priest is vested. He receives the stole, the sign of priestly office worn, like a yoke, across the shoulders. It is a 'yoke that is easy, a burden that is light' (Mt 11:30) not least because he has been made for this, and this for him, from all eternity. He receives the chasuble, a vestment that covers him entirely, giving an additional profile and purpose to his person. These things done, he now stands before us as a priest. As a new priest we welcome him.

With that welcome comes a new title. Now he is called 'Father'. This is a title of such respect as well as affection that it can cause real discomfort at first. No priest should ever think that the respect it denotes is his, personally, by right. It is due to him, befits him, only because of the gift he has received and the new relationship he has entered and embraced. There is indeed a mixture of pride and dread in every priest at the sound and implications of that title.

Yet this is a proper pride, for the ministry of the priest does indeed bring new life. He is a spiritual father. His words of absolution do bring forgiveness. His words of consecration do effect real change in the bread and wine placed upon the altar. They become the Body and Blood of Christ, the source of eternal life for all who receive them. Through the action of the priest they become the promise of our future glory.

There is dread in the title, too, for every priest is always conscious of the contrast between his calling and his humanity. He knows the real potential within himself for betrayal, for an abdication of the core values for which he now stands. If he should happen to forget this, then there are plenty of reminders, in the public forum, of the weaknesses and failures in the lives of priests. Every priest does well to remember this shared legacy of hurt that we have caused. It keeps fresh within us the truth of the axiom that the words and actions of a priest are doubly effective, both for good or for evil. Rudeness, sharpness seem all the more hurtful when coming from a priest. Ordinary kindness, too, can have an effect beyond normal reckoning.

The title 'Father' is a daily reminder of these things. It also reminds the priest that he is never to be at the centre of his own ministry. The title points always beyond the priest himself to the heavenly Father. Everything a priest does is to direct his people to the Father Himself. Just as the heart of Jesus was fixed on doing the Father's will, so too the heart of the priest, at one with Christ, has the same daily focus.

The outward expressions of the friendship with Christ which lie at the heart of priesthood are clear: the daily celebration of Mass, the work of being a minister of Word and Sacrament, caring for the people in the daily needs of life 'in the person of Christ, the Head'. The inner form of that friendship is different for each and every priest. The inner contours that unfold over the years, the emotional and spiritual impact of this bond are quite hidden. This relationship, like all others, is deeply personal. It cannot be fully expressed and certainly not fully understood by another. It is a unique 'one-to-one'.

In reflecting on the experience of this relationship every priest does well to remember how it all began. Each of us priests will have known the truth of the Gospel saying: 'You did not choose me, no I chose you.' (John 15:16) For each of us the coming of that insight will have been different; yet it is something we know in common. And it is an enormous reassurance! Whenever we feel a sense of pointlessness welling up within us in the face of the routine of life, these are words we should recall. When, as certainly happens, we doubt the rightness of the commitments we have given, this truth and our experience of it becomes a rock to which we can return. Already, in this ordination, we have heard an echo, a reaffirmation of this shared heritage. When presented with the candidate for ordination, I said these words:

'We rely on the help of the Lord God and our Saviour Jesus Christ, and we choose this man, our brother, for priesthood in the presbyterial order.'

These words give to every priest, young or old, a presumption of permanence in his vocation. They make clear that the origins of his vocation lie in the work of God and the discernment of the Church even if, for a while, he has lost sight of this. They are an invitation to perseverance, and they serve us well in the face of trouble and contrary attractions.

The words of Jesus in the Gospel of St John disclose the depth of this relationship: 'You are my friends... I do not call you servants anymore... I call you friends because I have made known to you everything I have learned from my Father.' (John 15:14-15) This is a relationship of real intimacy, a sharing of inner life, a relationship in which nothing is withheld. It is, from Christ's point of view, a relationship of perfect love.

From our point of view it is not quite thus! Our hearts are never as whole or entire. Our love is blemished. While the Lord may indeed make known everything to us, we are not capable of receiving it. If we were, we would live in profound peace. But we are not. So we experience confusion and unease. We are puzzled by the course of events and we struggle to find their meaning, their coherence with the promise of love on which we have built our hope.

No wonder a constant and favourite prayer for a priest is the prayer of Solomon. With him we pray for a heart that is discerning, one that is wise and shrewd. With Solomon we pray for wisdom so that all within us will be of God. Then we will be directed from within, towards that fullness of knowledge which befits the love already present within us:

> *'Send her (Wisdom) forth from the holy heavens, and from the throne of your glory send her that she may be with me and toil, and that I may learn what is pleasing to you; for she knows and understands all things, and she will guide me wisely in my actions and guard me with her glory.' (Wisdom 9:10)*

With such wisdom the priest will be more able to see and judge not only his own experience but also that of the people entrusted to his care. Such wisdom, which casts a true light on events, can help to reveal how and where God is at work. Similarly, such wisdom will also light up the ways when, in fact, we have strayed and are on the pathway of self-deceit.

A heart that is wise and shrewd is needed in every pastoral situation. It will guide us in the right way of teaching, helping us to find the well-judged word of encouragement or warning. Such a heart will help us to handle conflict, tragedy and bereavement with both sensitivity and genuine guidance.

Wisdom helps a priest to identify and shape a vocation in another: a vocation to marriage, to dedicated service, to religious life, to priesthood. A heart that is gifted with wisdom will help a priest to demonstrate and encourage prayer, in others and in his parish community. Quite simply, a heart that is wise and shrewd will see God in all things.

This becomes a very precious gift when, as priests, we begin to look back over our lives and our years of service. In doing this we need to be patient, humble and discerning, and ready to see the hand of God in everything. It is so easy not to do this for, in looking back, we can so often sense only failure and futility. But, with wisdom in our hearts, we can see how even failure, the personal failures of each one of us, have given rise to new strength, rather like a rich and abundant ivy growing on a broken wall. Perhaps we will be able to see how the inner tension with which we have lived, or the conflicts we have experienced, have brought forth a deeper purity within us, like two hands struggling together in the action of being washed clean.

As we look back over our lives as priests, on this day of an ordination, we strive to see how, in the Lord's providence, nothing is wasted. We sense that all has been put to good use, in and through the transforming love of Christ in which we have been rooted. Towards the end of his life, Bishop

Ullathorne, the first Bishop of Birmingham, wrote his own reflection on these experiences:

> *'We all have our shortcomings more or less; God knows them, and allows for them, for we are what we are, the poor, frail mortals in whom God works in the main his will and way. It is this contrast between what we are and what God does in us that fills us with hope and trust in his goodness.'*[1]

He certainly was blessed with a heart that was wise and shrewd!

Such is our prayer today, too. May this new priest grow to be a man deeply rooted in the Lord and therefore ready, in all humility, to be constantly searching out his way. Yes, we have found the One who fills our being with his love. Yet we know we do not possess him as he would wish to possess us. Ours is a long journey and, as priests, we make it both with and for our people. In accompanying them we will search for the truth of God in the tangled pathways of this life. This we will do in conversation and reflection, making careful and prudent use of our office of preaching to instruct and guide. In the faithful pastoral care we offer to our people, our constant search will be for the real and lasting love which is of God. We will be open in our life of prayer and in our search for the peace and beauty it can disclose. As priests, in our attentiveness to the sick, we shall help people to find the consolation which closer union with Christ can give. With the dying and bereaved we shall search out that promise of eternal life which alone can lighten that darkness.

The mark of the true disciple – and that is what a priest must always strive to be – is an unshakeable joy. This is not a constant happiness, which frankly lacks credibility, but a profound positive disposition, rooted in trust in God alone. That is the hallmark of a heart that is wise and shrewd. That is the fruit of the relationship of love with the Lord which ordination inaugurates and faithful ministry brings towards maturity. This is the true 'joy of priesthood' in which we rejoice today.

Notes

[1] *Letter to Genevieve Dupuis, 9 Dec 1888,*
William Bernard Ullathorne, Champ, Judith p492-3

Missioners

From the Gospel of St John

Jesus raised his eyes to heaven and said:

'Father, the hour has come: glorify your Son so that your Son may glorify you, and, through the power over all mankind that you have given him, let him give eternal life to those you have entrusted to him. And eternal life is this: to know you, the only true God, and Jesus Christ whom you have sent.

'Holy Father, keep those you have given me true to your name, so that they may be one like us. While I was with them, I kept those you had given me true to your name. I watched over them and not one is lost except the one who chose to be lost, and this was to fulfil the scriptures. But now I am coming to you and while still in the world I say these things to share my joy with them to the full. I passed your word on to them, and the world hated them, because they belong to the world no more than I belong to the world. I am not asking you to remove them from the world, but to protect them from the evil one. They do not belong to the world any more than I belong to the world. Consecrate them in the truth; your word is truth. As you sent me into the world, I have sent them into the world and for their sake I consecrate myself so that they too may be consecrated in truth.'

Chapter 17:1-3, 11-19

Consecrated in his Word

Based on the homily given at the Ordination to the Priesthood
of John Saward, St Aloysius, Oxford, 13 December 2003

There is something very special about an ordination which takes place during Advent. Each day we hear and reflect on passages of Scripture which speak to us of the promises of the Lord. He promises to be with us; to guard us in time of danger; to guide us, if we will let him, into the pathways of peace; to bring about his kingdom. Our hearts are constantly prompted to be awake to the coming of the Lord. We are conscious of a sense of growing expectation as the Feast of the Birth of the Lord approaches.

The promises which bring us such joy can also be spoken of as the promise of his blessing. The blessing of the Lord is his presence. His blessing, his presence springs from his desire to be with his people at every moment and circumstance. The blessing which God bestows upon us is, quite simply, his love. This blessing is an expression of God's delight in us, whether in the form of a rainbow, manna in the desert, a glimpse of the promised land or the bronze serpent raised up before the people to bring them life.

Advent is the season which restores in us this sense of God's presence and blessing. During it we can see again the goodness and loveliness of life in its essence: as a gift of a bountiful creator. During Advent we can refresh our appreciation of all that is precious to us, especially those we love. We can give them our blessing, words of joy in which all is referred to God and finds new strength and beauty in him. A parent's blessing of a child; the murmured, 'Good night and God bless you'; the prayerful wish for a safe journey are all ways in which we express our love while also bringing all we treasure to God, its true source and home. Our simple blessings are promises of lasting love, pointing to a future glory that is beyond ours to give. Advent is the season of promises and blessings. It is a good time for the ordination of a new priest.

St Bernard is a great teacher of how we are to live these days of Advent. He tutors us to be alert and attentive to the coming of the Lord in three ways.

He tells us that first is the coming of the Lord on earth, when the Second Person of the Blessed Trinity, the Eternal Word, took flesh and dwelt here in our midst. This coming, and the memory of it, is celebrated in these days of Advent, reaching a climax on Christmas Day itself. We tell and re-tell the story using carols, cribs, decorations and, of course, the witness of the Gospel.

The second coming of Christ lies ahead of us. He will come again, at the end of time, when 'all flesh shall see the salvation of our God'. Then Christ will bring the whole of creation to the fulfilment for which it longs, presenting it to his Eternal Father. This coming is made known to us in all the promises of the future kingdom to be found throughout the scriptures and, indeed, within the phrases of the Lord's prayer itself.

As St Bernard says:

'his first coming was in the flesh and in weakness... the last coming will be in glory and majesty.'[1]

Then St Bernard speaks of a third coming in these words:

'The other coming is hidden. In it, only the chosen see him within themselves and their souls are saved.'[2]

Here he is speaking of our daily life of faith, our prayer, our kindnesses, our patience and our compassion. He is asking us to see there the fruit of the presence of Christ living within each of us, even as he has promised.

St Bernard continues:

'This intermediary coming is like a road leading from the first to the last coming. In the first coming Christ was our redemption, in the last he will appear as our life, in this intermediary coming he is our rest and consolation. Do not imagine that what we are saying about the intermediary coming is simply our own fabrication. Listen to Christ himself: "If a man loves me he will keep my words, and my Father will love him, and we shall come to him".'[3]

So the task of Advent is clear. We are invited to welcome again the Word of God into our hearts, allowing that Word to *'pierce deep down into your innermost soul and penetrate your feelings and actions.'*[4] Each day in Advent we seek the Lord's presence more eagerly, attentive to his promptings, more generous in our response.

St Bernard's words include this wonderful promise: *'If you keep the word of God in this way without a doubt you will be kept by it.'*[5] The word will be our guide and guarantor. This is the road we travel, not one laid out by our own 'planning authority', but one established for us by God's loving providence. This road takes us from the present in which we bear *'the image of the earthly man'*[6], to a future *'when we shall bear the image of the heavenly man'*[7].

> *'Just as the old Adam was poured out throughout the whole man and filled him completely, so now let Christ take possession of the whole man, for he created the whole man, he redeemed the whole man and he will glorify the whole man.'*[8]

With these Advent thoughts to guide us we ponder the priestly prayer of Christ, in St John's Gospel, as a profound expression of the promises and blessings of God for us.

This is Jesus' prayer for his disciples. In it he lays bear the inner heart of discipleship.

Father, the hour has come:
Glorify your Son
so that your Son may glorify you;
and, through the power over all mankind that you have
given to him
let him give eternal life to all those you have entrusted
to him.
And eternal life is this:
to know you,
the only true God
and Jesus Christ whom you have sent. (John 17:1-3)

Knowledge of the Father is the heart of Jesus. The Father is the focus of his longing, just as obedience to the will of the Father is the expression of that love. But Jesus' love for his Father, like all human loving, must be tested and purified. He comes to express that love most fully in the words spoken in the garden and from the cross. 'Let your will be done, not mine.' (Luke 22:43) and 'Father, into your hands I commend my spirit.' (Luke 23:46)

So too the disciple's heart is focused on the Father. The disciple knows the name of the Father and has been taught to speak to God as 'Abba'. Faithfulness to this relationship is the deepest longing of every follower of Jesus, and in that desire the disciple knows that Jesus is a constant companion and leader. If the disciple stays close to Jesus then this relationship with the Father is secure. This is the fruit of Jesus' prayer, his promise to us.

The prayer of Jesus continues:

> *'I passed your word on to them*
> *and the world hated them,*
> *because they belong to the world*
> *no more than I belong to the world.*
> *I am not asking you to remove them from the world,*
> *but to protect them from the evil one.*
> *They do not belong to the world*
> *any more than I belong to the world.*
> *Consecrate them in the truth;*
> *your word is truth.*
> *As you sent me into the world*
> *I have sent them into the world*
> *and for their sake I consecrate myself*
> *so that they too may be consecrated in truth."*
> *(John 17:14-19)*

This is the programme of discipleship. What is to take place in us is the unfolding of the relationship with the Father and the Son. And this relationship is seen and lived in the life of Jesus, in his mission in the world. The course of our discipleship is the 'mystery of his purpose, the hidden plan he so kindly made in Christ from the beginning to act upon when the times had run their course to the end.' (Ephesians 1:9) We are to be 'consecrated' in that Word, that Truth, and that alone can bring our human nature to its fulfilment.

Jesus' prayer makes clear that this consecration will bring heartache and suffering, for so many of its demands are at odds with the expectations 'of the world'. While the Word is certainly the fulfilling of the promise, how this is to be achieved is neither immediately obvious nor congenial. A battle is to be engaged, for our human nature is not fully attuned to God's purposes. Indeed, as each one of us knows, the pathway of discipleship, of 'doing the Father's will', involves a great deal of self-denial, foregoing of immediate satisfaction and a generosity of spirit.

Such actions are, of course, inspired by love. It is love alone that makes the way of discipleship possible. The more we realise that God's love for us knows no limits then the more our love, given in return, can be generous, unstinting and enduring.

Jesus' prayer asks the Father to keep us true to his Word so that our discipleship may be fruitful. We know that the Word in which we are consecrated, which marks out our path, is none other than Christ himself. Quite simply, God's plan is a person. So our journey of discipleship, its programme, is itself an unfolding relationship. The pathway of self-denial is, in fact, an unfolding of intimacy with Christ. What stands opposed to 'the world' and 'to the evil one' is not an alternative philosophy, or another set of values, but a person who not only embodies the truth but invites us to discover and live it as a relationship with himself.

Christ's consecration, about which he prays, is death on the cross. In this death Christ not only displays the truth of all human living but also invites us all to know him in that love. His consecration, his sacrifice, is also and always a banquet opening for us all the glory that is his 'as the only Son of the Father, full of grace and truth.' (John 1:14)

In unfolding the promises and blessings of God in this way, the Gospel of John leads us to understand the great gift of priesthood given to the Church. Through the irrevocable effects of ordination, the priest is bound to Christ in a particular way, precisely in the terms of this priestly prayer. The priest becomes one with Christ in the constant and all-embracing prayer offered to the Father on behalf of the Church. The priest and Christ are one in the action of Christ's sacrificial death by which he is consecrated and glorified. The priest is one with Christ in the nurturing, or 'watching over' the disciples who, like their Master, are sent on mission into the world, even in the face of 'the evil one'.

The priest fulfils these tasks of prayer, sacrifice and pastoral care as a minister of Christ, as one who makes the promised companionship of Christ both visible and effective. The priest is both a 'minister of the Word' and a 'minister of the sacraments' for these are the ways in which Christ fulfils his promise and gives us his blessing.

The priest, then, accompanies his people in their journey of discipleship. He urges them to deepen their relationship with Christ, to seek his forgiveness for their sin, to know his compassion in their need and to draw on his unwavering love as the source of their self-sacrifice. Serving the holiness of the people is the heart of the ministry of the priest.

The priest fulfils these tasks only and always as a member of the diocesan presbyterate, or bound in some other way to the visible life of the Church. The promise of obedience made by the priest underpins this bond and assures the people that the ministry they receive from their priest is not simply the product of his own imagining or learning but truly the plan of the Father, entrusted to Christ and through him to his Body, the Church. This is the context in which every priest exercises his ministry.

But let us return to St Bernard, for his threefold understanding of the coming of Christ also provides a framework in which the priest can enter more deeply into his ministry.

First among the duties of the priest is the proclamation of Christ, the Incarnate Word. Wherever the priest is seen, he is recognised as 'a man of God' and, more particularly, a man of Jesus Christ. Our visible presence is a statement of the importance of Christ. Perhaps that is why we priests can sometimes feel uncomfortable in public. We are, at times, a provocation and, at times, the object of the frustration and cynicism of others. Fundamentally our presence is a claim about an enduring truth which is not susceptible to personal opinion or control. To this extent we are an irritant in today's culture. For if Christ is indeed the Eternal Word then Christ is a sign of contradiction to a world which wants to create, and recreate, all things in its own fashion.

This proclamation of the unchanging truth of Christ becomes credible when it is experienced as also being the proclamation of the unchanging love of God, in Christ, for all. Love gives Christian witness its credibility. And this applies to the life of the priest and the people.

So our proclamation of Christ is a constant unfolding of the mystery of Christ who is truth, who is love, and justice, and salvation, and hope, and joy, and beauty. Only slowly are 'first impressions' broken down to reveal the Gospel's saving truth.

It is, of course, the task of the priest to present and teach the dogmas of the Church as the 'saving truths' they are. Time and again, in ways suited to the age, circumstances and capacity of our listeners, we are to present all the implications of that first coming of Christ. We are to speak of the promises and events that led up to it, of the detailed words and actions given to us by Christ, and explain the long, rich tradition of reflection on his time on earth which has flowed from that 'fullness of time'. (Hebrews 1:2)

An important part of this task of teaching is to keep alive the promise of his second coming. In the midst of all the pressures of daily living this promise is so crucial. We can so easily lose sight of its calming perspective. In this promise we are assured that all things will be brought to their fulfilment. In its light, our efforts, our trials, our suffering are, in comparison, short-lived. Our ultimate future is secure.

A crucial testimony to this promise of the second coming of Christ is, of course, the virtue of hope. We priests must offer evidence of such hope in our own lives. Somehow the sight of a troubled, anxious, deeply unsettled priest is worrying. I remember one forthright woman saying to me when I was in such a state: 'You shouldn't be like that. You have your "book" each day!' She meant the breviary and she was reminding me that, if I were truly rooted in prayer, I would manage my anxieties quite differently.

If that is the true effect of daily prayer then it is even more true of the celebration of the Mass. Here we come to the fullest proclamation of the promise of heaven, and of the fulfilment of all things in Christ. In him all our efforts at prayer find their fulfilment. In him the promised ending of our earthly pilgrimage is made clear. Those who have died are brought 'to share in his supper'. In him, day by day, we too are given the promise of our future destiny. In Christ on the cross we celebrate the truth of the glory of our humanity. In the humanity of Christ, lifted high in his resurrection from the dead, we see the destiny of our own humanity. This is a promise of such clarity and power! In that promise we strive to live each day.

Living and serving the third coming of Christ also lies at the heart of priestly ministry. This, as St Bernard described, is the road we travel day by day. This third coming of Christ is made up of the hidden, working presence of Christ, through the Holy Spirit, in our daily lives. By this coming he slowly fashions us, conforming us to his likeness, if we let him, until we are fit for his kingdom. Nothing is beyond his scope and influence. When we are weighed down by the ordinariness of daily routines, or when we are beside ourselves with delight, or when we are surprised by unexpected love, or when we are rendered speechless with frustration or pain, then the Lord, in the power of the Holy Spirit, can be preparing us to be more fully his dwelling place.

The task of the priest is to minister to this process. He, along with many others, is in a position to accompany his people on this journey of faith. Here the pastoral priest will always be in Advent mode: attentive, listening, sensitively responsive. When listening to the experiences of the people, the priest is attuned to the work of the Lord. He will be focused on how these events might open each person a little more to the compassionate and loving presence of God. He will, of course, attend to what is being said, but he will also be listening to another more silent story.

The skilful priest, in the fashion of Advent, will not say too much. He will not make the running, preferring to allow the picture to unfold. With difficulty, at times, he will resist the temptation to provide quick answers or merely pious responses, but with a real deference to the importance of what is being presented he will tread lightly and sensitively. He is serving the saving presence of the Lord and will do so in all humility.

The ordination ceremony portrays the ways in which the priest is prepared and equipped for this ministry. The prayer of ordination and the anointing of hands are the outward signs of that inner gift of the Holy Spirit by which this ministry is given its roots in Christ Himself. The invocation of the saints make it clear that the priest has at his side the company of heaven. His ministry is always that of the entire Church. The vestments he receives remind us all that the priest is never simply himself. Of course he is always to remain himself and be true to himself. But that self is now taken up into a greater identity which will refine and fulfil the personal self of the priest. We can say this only because, at this point, we are confident that God has called the man to the priesthood. It was for this he was made. No violence is done to him in following this calling, in this ordination. Rather, here his deepest personality is fulfilled. Now the new priest is truly himself, free to put behind him any uncertainty, free to consecrate himself wholeheartedly to the work of the Lord, free to sing the praises of God in the company of the Church.

For this fulfilment and for this consecration we give great thanks today. May the heavenly Father bless this new priest and lead him, through his Word, to the fullness of joy and the happiness of heaven. Amen.

Notes

[1] *St Bernard, Sermon 5 on Advent, The Divine Office I*: Office of Readings, Advent Week I, Wednesday, p61

[2] Ibid

[3] Ibid

[4] Ibid

[5] Ibid, p62

[6] Ibid

[7] Ibid

[8] Ibid

Missioners

From the Prophet Jeremiah

The word of Yahweh was addressed to me, saying
'Before I formed you in the womb I knew you;
before you came to birth I consecrated you;
I have appointed you as prophet to the nations.'
I said, 'Ah, Lord Yahweh; look, I do not know how to speak:
I am a child!"
But Yahweh replied,
'Do not say, "I am a child".
Go now to those to whom I send you
and say whatever I command you.
Do not be afraid of them,
for I am with you to protect you -
it is Yahweh who speaks!'
Then Yahweh put out his hand and touched my mouth and said to
me:
'There! I am putting my words into your mouth.
Look, today I am setting you
over nations and over kingdoms,
to tear up and to knock down,
to destroy and to overthrow,
to build and to plant.'

Chapter 1:4-10

Purify my Heart

Based on the homily given at the Diaconate Ordinations,
St Mary's College, Oscott, 19 June 2004

This ordination is taking place on the Feast of the Immaculate Heart of Mary. Today we join with her in praising God for all his good gifts. In particular we thank God for our deacons and priests. We pray that they may be close to Mary in their attentiveness to the Lord and in their readiness to proclaim his goodness, day by day. We pray, too, that each of us may come away from this celebration with hearts renewed.

Isaiah sings of the works of the Lord. So too does Mary. So we read Isaiah's words with Mary in mind.

'My people will be famous throughout the nations, their descendants throughout the peoples. All who see them will admit that they are a race whom the Lord has blessed. I exult for joy in the Lord, my soul rejoices in my God, for he has clothed me in the garments of salvation, he has wrapped me in the cloak of integrity, like a bridegroom wearing his wreath, like a bride adorned with her jewels. For as the earth makes fresh things grow, as a garden makes seeds spring up, so will the Lord make both integrity and praise spring up in the sight of the nations.' (Isaiah 61:9-11)

Here we find one of the tributaries which flowed into Mary's great *Magnificat*. Her voice praises God for 'the marvels the Lord has worked for me' (Luke 1:48), resonating the voice of Hannah (1 Samuel 2:1-10) and, we trust, our voices too. These are voices raised in praise of God's work, the fruitfulness of grace, the showing forth of the gifts of the Holy Spirit.

Yet it is the last sentence of this passage on which we can reflect most closely. The work of the Lord, in the image of the garden, will 'make both integrity and praise spring up in the sight of the nations.' (Isaiah 61:11)

Integrity and praise are closely coupled in this promise. They are intrinsically linked together, inseparable in the abundance of the garden.

Our experience illustrates this. Can a person who lacks integrity really give praise? Is it not true that real, thorough praise will flow only from a heart no longer seeking to satisfy its own desires or struggling with its own demons? A cynical person doesn't really give praise to another, not at least until that cynicism has been overcome or suspended.

Our prayer of praise is so often fractured by the anger we feel about this or that perceived injustice. We have to get over our anger with God before we can truly praise him. Ambiguity in our inner selves disrupts our prayer and distorts the praise we give to another or to God himself.

Of course we struggle for integrity. We seek that wholeness of self which seems so elusive and, at times, only fleetingly enjoyed. Occasionally we sense that we have 'got ourselves together'. Yet even underneath that emotional equilibrium we shall always sense the deeper dichotomies of sin. We do not always do what is called for by our inner self. We are not thoroughly the person we would wish to be. Indeed our finest praise may well spring to our lips when we know we have been forgiven, and our integrity repaired.

So there is no perfect praise without integrity. Similarly there is no true integrity that does not give rise to real praise. We know that the integrity we seek will always be a gift of the Lord. It lies ahead of us. It is not some initial gift which we have lost. Children may have greater spontaneity than we adults, but they too struggle with temptations to wrongdoing, they too manipulate, seek to hide and deceive. At times, they do not know what they truly want. Integrity is a gift that comes with maturity.

Integrity is the fruit of grace. It is acquired inasmuch as we cooperate with the Lord and strive to live a life based on virtue, especially the virtues of humility and honesty. No amount of introspection, by itself, will ever produce the wholeness for which we long. Coming to a deeper understanding of our inner self, with all our complex or hidden motives, our self-deception and our inherited burdens, helps a great deal. Such knowledge lays out before us the task. But true integrity will be achieved only with the grace of God and with time.

Mary enjoyed that integrity in a unique way. She had the inner wholeness and freedom for which we all yearn. That is why she could say, with total integrity: 'I am the handmaid of the Lord. Let what you have said be done to me.' (Luke 1:38) She possessed herself so utterly that she could give herself totally. Sin had not troubled her. From this integrity sprang her perfect praise, expressed in the *Magnificat*.

For these reasons we speak of the Immaculate Heart of Mary and recognise her as a worthy dwelling place for the Lord. She was formed and grew under the influence of the Holy Spirit, 'wrapped in the cloak of integrity' and 'famous throughout the nations'. Today we ask her intercession that *'we may become a more worthy temple of your glory.'* (Opening Prayer)

One of the hymns we use today express this prayer:

'Purify my heart;
Let me be as gold or precious silver;
Refiner's fire,
My one desire
To be holy, set apart,
Ready to do your will.'

The desires expressed in this hymn are at the centre of discipleship. We long to be close to the Lord, to let nothing separate us from him. We want to hold ourselves ready, as fully as we can, to do his will. We seek that purity of heart which sees the end of ambiguity and of inauthenticity in our thoughts and actions.

How is the work to be achieved? What are the means used by the Lord to draw us on towards this eventual goal of a pure heart? How are we to shape and mark each day so that it is truly a step on this conscious journey to integrity and faith?

There are so many ways and means by which the work of grace is carried out. Today we focus on those put before us in the ordinations of deacons and priests. They are to be 'conformed to Christ' by this sacrament. Their hearts are to be purified in the working of this sacrament so that their ministry may be fruitful and truly an instrument of grace for others. How will the grace of this ministry purify their hearts?

By ordination, priests and deacons become 'Heralds of the Gospel'. Here is a testing ground of the heart. This call, and the demands it makes, contains within it the ways in which hearts will be made pure.

Every person called to proclaim the Word of God will experience this purification. Every prophet of the Old Testament bears witness to this. Jeremiah is a fine example. His call makes clear the ways in which being a herald of the Word of God will purify the heart of those who give themselves to that task. (Jeremiah 1:4-10)

To begin with the deacon and priest must heed the first phrase of Jeremiah's summons: 'Go now to those to whom I send you.' (v.7)

His purpose in life is no longer one that the priest or deacon shapes for himself. He is called and sent. In a way which our age finds quite scandalous, the deacon and priest hand over to another crucial decisions about their lives. They promise obedience to the Lord in and through the Church. Now, like every prophet before them, they will find themselves in places not of their own choosing, and in situations they would rather avoid. This is a real testing of motive and desire. It is a genuine purifying of the heart.

The deacon and the priest, indeed every disciple, now stand under a new kind of judgement. The one to whom they are accountable is the one by whom they have been sent. This is the key judgement about which they must be concerned. Their thoughts and actions are never hidden from the Lord and it is to him that they must give their account. The bar of public opinion is not important. Nor is the judgement of their peers.

Yet it is so difficult not to live by and for popular affirmation. Constantly we seek the approval of those around us because that approval plays such an important part in shoring up our fragile self-esteem. Yet the one judgement which matters is not to be found there. Only slowly will our hearts attune to this new pattern of approval, encouragement and inner peace. These come from the Lord, also mediated in the Church as best we can. This, too, is a radical purifying of the heart.

The next words of Jeremiah's call are equally demanding: 'Say whatever I command you.' (v.5)

Slowly every deacon and priest has to loosen the grip of their desire to be heralds of their own opinions. Of course they will be full of bright ideas and of their own experience and stories. But each of those stories and experiences needs to be rigorously tested to see if it faithfully conveys a full Gospel message. Often the desire to speak of self, to draw attention to self, overcomes the duty of being faithful to the authentic Gospel. The use of experience and illustration can be ways of integrating the Gospel into everyday living, but this requires a real purity of heart. It requires the conscious intention of truly being one with 'the mind of the Church', from whom the Gospel is received and in whose name it is proclaimed.

To seek to serve the Gospel in conformity with the Church also brings to its herald the sureness of knowing that what is being said is indeed true. The deacon and priest can sincerely say: 'Here is a truth to live by.' No longer does the disciple have to be paying constant attention to spin and focus groups in order to find a bearing in a value-free world. The truth of the Gospel is a rock on which to build. To live by the command of the Lord gives a sound framework for freedom. Of course, popular opinion is not to be ignored. It is important for sensing and sharing the ebb and flow of concerns and moods. But it is not a foundation for living. In fact it imprisons the heart. Adherence to the Gospel gives a freedom and purity to all we do.

The next words heard by Jeremiah take us to the core of our struggle. 'Do not be afraid for I am with you to protect you.' (v.8)

There are good reasons for the deacon and the priest, and the disciple too, to be fearful. In stepping forward into the limelight of the world and of public opinion, each will feel vulnerable. We know only too well how the failures of each of us weaken our corporate effort. Some of these failures are very public indeed. Others are less well known. Others are quite hidden. Yet each in its own way leads to a weakening of the body. This is a real anxiety.

So, too, is the open hostility that we experience as heralds of the Gospel. This hostility may not take the form of physical assault, supported by force or law, but there is a real hostility of view and argument on the part of some. For them religious faith is, simply, a 'bad thing', and British society would be better off without it. Virtue is scorned and even the quest for wholeness cynically dismissed. Often we can feel helpless before this attack, just as we can feel ill-equipped for the technical arguments put forward by advancing science in key moral questions.

But we are not to be afraid. Slowly our hearts are tutored in the humility that is needed to know that we are not meant to be self-reliant. Slowly we learn to be dependent on the Lord. He says 'I am with you to protect you'. (v.8) We gradually learn the truth of these words and the many ways in which they are fulfilled.

One of the ways in which this promise is fulfilled is through his continuing presence in the Church. By baptism we become grafted into the vibrant tree of faith. Through ordination, a deacon and a priest become part of an Order: the order of deacons, the presbyterate of the diocese. The working out of these new bonds are ways in which our hearts are gradually purified of the individualism which they acquire because of the environment of our life and growth.

In the life of faith we learn, in practice, that we do not stand alone in our desire to proclaim the Gospel. We come to appreciate the importance of being part of a family of faith and of being open to that family, and faithful to it as well. The deacon or priest who keeps his distance from his fellow deacons and priests, or who is highly selective in the company he keeps, is not allowing the Lord to be with him according to all the patterns through which that promise is fulfilled. His heart is still shaped and led by an individualism which pays high regard to its own needs and desires rather than to those among whom he has been sent and placed. We need to overcome these self-centred instincts if we are to allow God to do this work through us. The pathway towards purity of heart is demanding and steep.

In our journey we look to Mary. Perhaps we see the purity of her heart most clearly at the foot of the cross. There, despite the heartache, she opens herself to be one with her son. There, in desolation, we see the Immaculate Heart of Mary in all the splendour of her selfless love.

For her Son's part too, we see the fullness of his Sacred Heart most clearly in his death on the cross. At that moment, St John tells us, 'One of the soldiers pierced his side with a lance; and immediately there came out blood and water.' (John 19:34) His heart is emptied for our sake, giving forth the Holy Spirit which is the fountain of all grace. At that moment Mary, too, is conformed entirely to the will of the Father. There she is free, pure, undefiled by anger or bitterness, entirely one with her Son. But the road is hard.

Today's Gospel passage helps us to understand that road and how far back it stretched. We heard a narrative from the infancy of Jesus. We read of Jesus remaining behind in the Temple and becoming separated from Joseph and Mary. We heard her natural maternal feeling breaking forth in the heartfelt words:

'My child why have you done this to us? See how worried your father and I have been, looking for you.' (Luke 2:48)

We know that Mary 'stored up all these things in her heart' (v.52). They must surely have come back to her as she stayed and suffered at the foot of the cross. This is the Father's business.

Now we can see the pathway towards purity of heart. It is the pathway of obedience, that readiness always to listen, to put self aside, to give way in order to be filled. This obedience, this readiness to listen, takes a very particular form in the life of the deacon and the priest. They promise obedience to the bishop, for the good of the Church.

For all disciples, too, there is the 'obedience of faith', that readiness to put our own will in second place, to allow our instinctive desires to be shaped by the Holy Spirit active within us. Only then, and as a gift of the Lord, will we find the integrity for which we are made. Only then will we praise the Lord in fullness and freedom. This, we know, is our final destiny. For now we accompany and serve each other as we long for the work of God to be carried out among us.

Missioners

From the Prophet Zechariah

An oracle. The word of Yahweh about Israel. It is Yahweh who speaks, who spread out the heaven and founded the earth and formed the spirit of man within him:

'Look, I am going to make Jerusalem an intoxicating cup to all the surrounding peoples...'

'When that day comes, I mean to make Jerusalem a stone to be lifted by all the peoples; all who try to lift it will hurt themselves severely.

When that day comes I mean to make the clans of Judah like a brazier burning in a pile of wood, like a flaming torch in stubble, and they will consume the peoples round them to right and left. And Jerusalem shall stand firm in her place.

'When that day comes, I shall set myself to destroy all the nations who advance against Jerusalem. But over the House of David and the citizens of Jerusalem I will pour out a spirit of kindness and prayer. They will look on the one whom they have pierced; they will mourn for him as for an only son, and weep for him as people weep for a first-born child. When that day comes, there will be a great mourning in Judah, like the mourning of Hadad-rimmon in the plain of Megiddo.....'

'When that day comes, a fountain will be opened for the House of David and the citizens of Jerusalem, for sin and impurity'.

Chapter 12:1-3, 6, 9-12; 13:1

Kindness and Prayer

Based on the homily given at the Ordination to the Priesthood

of Alexander Master, St Aloysius, Oxford, 20 June 2004

T he Prophet Zechariah speaks of the deliverance and restoration of Jerusalem. His words express the long cherished hope of the people: that all will be well. This hope is founded on trust in God, the God who shows himself to be both merciful and just, both kind and severe. This prophecy, in two short sentences, takes us to the core of God's dealing with his people and to the fulfilment of his promises.

> *'Over the House of David and the citizens of Jerusalem I will pour out a spirit of kindness and prayer. They will look on the one whom they have pierced; they will mourn for him as for an only son and weep for him as people weep for a firstborn child.' (Zechariah 12:10-11)*

These two sentences, with the complex connection between them, are a rich source of reflection for us as we ponder the gift of priesthood and the ministry of the priest today.

It is not difficult to see how these words of Zechariah find their fulfilment in Christ. All the promises made to Israel are gradually revealed as leading to an unexpected Messiah. He, the one from Nazareth, bears on his shoulders the mantle of this inheritance. In him the words of the prophets are fulfilled.

We know this in our experience of faith. He is the one from whom we seek 'kindness and prayer'. We turn to him when our hearts are weary, remembering his gracious invitation: 'Come to me all you who labour and are overburdened and I will give you rest.' (Matthew 11:28) He promises 'rest for our souls'. So we open our hearts to him who is 'the loving kindness of our God' (Luke 1:78) and receive from him, in all gentleness and humility, the comfort and consolation for which we long.

We know from our experience of faith that we can turn to him for the gift of prayer too. We echo the words of the first disciples when they said: 'Lord, teach us how to pray.' (Luke 11:1) We too come to him to receive instruction, to hear the words we are to use in prayer: 'Our Father'. He is the one who is both the source and the channel of all our prayer. From him comes the desire to praise the Father, the words with which to do so and the means by which we know our prayer is heard.

In ways such as these Jesus calls us to himself. He is for us utterly attractive for he is the source of our peace and of our joy. We come to him in all our needs and find in him our satisfaction.

He leads us unfailingly, as does the Church, to the well-springs of that consolation and satisfaction. The source is the Holy Spirit, the Comforter. The Spirit, who is the love of Father and Son, pours into our hearts all the fulfilment we desire.

This Holy Spirit is the soul's most delightful guest who can soften our hardness of heart, melt our glacial moods and bend our obstinate self-centredness.

The gift of the Holy Spirit, we know, comes to us in redeeming fullness from the death of Christ on the cross. It was there that He 'yielded up his spirit' (John 19:30) so that the same Spirit could flood the world with the possibility of 'kindness and prayer'.

So we must look upon the one whom we have pierced if we are to receive that same 'spirit of kindness and prayer'. Only by looking on Christ on the cross can we come to know the depth of his kindness. His love is complete. His kindness towards us knows no bounds. His giving is total, and it is for each of us. This is the true and full 'spirit of kindness'. Here we see God's compassion for all people, the gift of forgiving love. This is its source and its price.

Here, too, we see the true character of prayer. In Christ, prayer to the Father is not simply a matter of words, nor even of desire. His prayer is expressed by his action, the action of an entire life. This is a prayer beyond words, one that rises from the very depth of his being, the eternal depth of his being. He, the only Son of the Father, is entirely one with the Father, from all time. Once, in the splendour of truth, this eternal praise and love is expressed in our flesh. In this moment all the aspirations of our prayer are made clear. What as yet lies hidden in the depth of our being, for we are children of the same Father, is suddenly made plain. We, like Christ, are fulfilled once we can present ourselves, entirely, to the Father in actions of praise and love. That is what our daily prayer seeks to express. Even though it is weak, fleeting and never entire, the nature of our prayer, of all prayer, seeks that fullness. We find it in Christ, in him in whom the 'spirit of prayer' is truly to be found.

We must be willing, then, to gaze on our crucified saviour and to embrace him. If not, then how can we be filled with the Spirit which flows from his wounded side? If we turn away, then we distance ourselves from the very gift we are seeking. Of course the sight of Christ in the agony of death is distressing. We should not flinch from it. Instead we should recognise our part in contributing to the burden of distorted love which Christ is bearing and refashioning. We too can 'mourn for him and weep for him as people weep for a first-born child.' (v.10)

When we weep for him our hearts are softened to receive his Spirit. Then our hearts can be filled with this kindness. Then our prayer truly becomes united to his. It becomes part of his perfect prayer of the Cross and most certainly reaches the throne of our heavenly Father.

'I will pour out a spirit of kindness and prayer. They will look on the one whom they have pierced.' (v.10)

These are the mysteries ministered by the priest. Every priest is ordained to be one through whose ministry that spirit is again made available to all people. He is the one to whom are entrusted the sacred mysteries through which we can again look upon the one whom we have pierced. Through the actions of the priest God fulfils his promises.

Every time Mass is celebrated we come again to Calvary. As the priest stands at the altar, his hands raised in prayer in a gesture which reflects the outstretched arms of Christ on the cross, so we all stand at the foot of that cross as truly as if we were present on Golgotha. Here we can gaze on the one whom we have pierced.

Through the action of the priest the sacrifice of Christ is renewed. His body is broken in the reality of his sacramental presence. His blood is poured out. They are held, elevated before us, so that we can indeed see him, be drawn to him, open our hearts to him.

We know, too, that from these life-giving wounds come the streams of living water. From them the Holy Spirit is again poured over the world. That Spirit is the spirit of kindness, of humility, of love. That Spirit draws us again to the Father with new attentiveness. That Spirit renews in us the desire to be kind to one another and gives us the strength, the grace, to be so. Whenever we celebrate Mass together that Spirit is renewed within us and we glimpse the prospect of laying aside all bitterness and discord and of living in harmony as children of one Lord.

These streams of living water also give us the spirit of true prayer. The Spirit moves us not only to praise God for and in all things but also raises our hearts to pray on behalf of all others. Under the influence of the Holy Spirit, our prayer ranges widely, including not just those we love or who have asked for our prayers, but countless others whose faces we do not know but who stand in need of that same comforting Spirit. We pray for the sick, the lonely, the imprisoned. We pray for peace in distant lands and for justice in conflicts which of ourselves we cannot influence at all. But, as we gaze on the one from whom the Spirit of all prayer comes forth, we can pray for all humanity, in all our desperate needs.

It is the immense privilege of the priest to be the one whose hands and voice are used by Christ to make present again this gift of the Holy Spirit. The priest gathers together the prayers of the people and raises them to the Father, through, with and in Christ. This is the climax of the central Eucharistic prayer of every celebration of Mass.

Kindness and Prayer

At this point, the altar of sacrifice, the altar from which our prayer has risen, becomes the table of our banquet, the place we are fed, blessed and nourished with the life-giving Spirit. Here, too, the priest is the one who, in the name of Christ, summons us to the feast. He holds before us the Body and Blood of Christ now to be gazed upon as our most treasured gift. He whom we have pierced comes to us as our food and drink. He becomes our life-blood. We become his flesh. In him we now live and move and have our being.

Every priest, as admonished on the day of his ordination, is to be faithful to the mysteries he celebrates. We priests must never fail to gaze on Christ ourselves. As priests we must never avert our eyes from him. We should never turn away from his pain, his agony, his death. In like manner as priests we should never distance ourselves from the distress and suffering of the people in our care. It is easy to do so. As priests we are tempted by the appeal of a 'professional status', giving us a kind of immunity from the personal sufferings of others. We can be tempted to fulfil our ministry in a detached and professional manner. Yet we are pastors, not professionals. We care for our people with the eyes of Christ and see in their hardship a sharing in the sufferings of Christ. That is never a matter of cool distance for us. Of course we do not enter with personal emotion into the lives of our people. But we speak with them, stand with them in the unique manner of the priest, as the one in their midst who is a spiritual father.

The instinct by which people bring their troubles to us priests is a right and proper instinct. They do not come expecting solution or cure. They come expecting kindness and prayer, those fruits of the Spirit on which we have been reflecting. As priests we seek to draw from the pain or distress of those before us that openness of heart which can give rise to a more profound dependence on Christ. This can only be done effectively if we ourselves live by that dependence. The self-sufficient priest can lead people only to himself. No salvation is to be found there. When we priests know our dependence on Christ, acknowledging that he is the source of our kindness and prayer, then we can lead others to him.

Today we pray for newly ordained priests, that their ministry will be fruitful, just as their discipleship is faithful. We pray, too, for all priests, that their celebration of Mass will renew within them the spirit of kindness and prayer. The fruit of that spirit will lead many to the Lord.

Missioners

From the Letter to the Hebrews

Every high priest has been taken out of mankind and is appointed to act for men in their relations with God, to offer gifts and sacrifices for sins; and so he can sympathise with those who are ignorant or uncertain because he too lives in the limitations of weakness. That is why he has to make sin offerings for himself as well as for the people. No one takes this honour on himself, but each one is called by God, as Aaron was. Nor did Christ give himself the glory of becoming high priest, but he had it from the one who said to him: You are my son, today I have become your father, and in another text: You are a priest of the order of Melchizedek, and for ever. During his life on earth, he offered up prayer and entreaty, aloud and in silent tears, to the one who had the power to save him out of death, and he submitted so humbly that his prayer was heard. Although he was Son, he learnt to obey through suffering; but having been made perfect, he became for all who obey him the source of eternal salvation and was acclaimed by God with the title of high priest of the order of Melchizedek.

Chapter 5:1-10

Hands of the Priest

*Based on the homily given at the Ordination to the Priesthood
of Richard Scott, Our Lady and All Saints, Stourbridge,
18 December 2004*

The Letter to the Hebrews is full of reflection on the priesthood of Christ. It explores the contrast between the old and new priesthood, drawing out the radical newness of Christ which does not simply fulfil the old but far surpasses it.

The passage on which we ponder today (Hebrews 5:1-10) highlights two aspects of the priesthood of Christ, the priesthood which we celebrate at this ordination. In the first place it makes it clear that no man appoints himself to be a priest. No one can declare themselves to be a priest of Jesus Christ.

'No one takes this honour on himself, but each one is called by God, as Aaron was. Nor did Christ give himself the glory of becoming high priest, but he had it from the one who said to him: "You are my son, today I have become your father."'
(Hebrews 5:5)

It is the Father alone who appoints those who share in the priesthood of Christ and the Father alone who grants them the gift of the Holy Spirit.

Then, in the second place, this passage also makes clear the fact that this priesthood, given by the Father, does not wipe out our weaknesses nor, somehow, enable us to transcend them. Rather we live with our human weaknesses and failures in and through this priesthood. They become part of our priesthood. Indeed they become a crucial part of it.

'During his life on earth, he offered up prayer and entreaty, aloud and in silent tears, to the one who had the power to save him out of death, and he submitted so humbly that his prayer was heard. Although he was Son, he learned to obey through suffering.' (v.7-8)

These two features of the high priesthood of Christ are most certainly true of our participation in it.

Indeed, reflection on priesthood during this time of Advent gives additional emphasis to the initiative of the Father and the self-emptying of the Son. We are taught by St Paul that Christ Jesus 'emptied himself to assume the condition of a slave' becoming entirely as we are in our humanity (Philippians 2:6-7). It is precisely in this humble state, not clinging to his equality with God, that he was 'raised on high' and appointed High Priest from the cross, by the will of the Father. In none of this, never in the unfolding of salvation, did Christ fulfil his own will. The struggle to be conformed to the will of the Father lay at the heart of his agony, his passion, in the garden. Our redemption is born from this handing over of his entire self to the Father. This made the prayers of his priesthood so fruitful. Only in this way did he become 'the source of eternal salvation and was acclaimed by God with the title of high priest according to the order of Melchizedeck.' (v.10)

There are many signs of this priesthood in our ordination ceremony today. In word and action we seek to focus not only on the action of the Father and the self-giving of the new priest but also on how this inner core of the mystery of salvation is present in the life of each one of us. I would like to reflect on just one of these actions, the anointing with chrism, which takes place in a few moments.

This anointing is a rich sign. It gives outward expression to the action of God, an action which picks out the one being anointed and gives to that person a particular calling. This anointing, as we know, imparts a character, or seal, on the inner being of a person, on his soul. It is an irrevocable mark of God's ownership, and of the task, or mission, that is being handed over at this moment.

The anointing is always given within the Church, indeed, through the Church. No one can appoint himself to be a priest. The anointing must be received through the ministry of one who has already been appointed and anointed for that task. Both the chrism itself, blessed and given its power through the Liturgy of the Church, and the minister who employs it, are gifts of the Father, given through Christ and his visible body, the Church.

But before we come to that moment of priestly anointing it is good to recall that all who have been baptised have also been anointed with chrism. Each one is thereby bound to Christ in a particular fashion. Indeed when Jesus speaks of 'those you have given to me' (John 17:12) he is speaking of every baptised person. In our baptism, by which we are drawn into the life of God in a sacramental way, the Father is placing us into the hands of his beloved Son, entrusting us to him. So when Jesus assures the disciples that he will 'lose nothing' of all he has been given, he is speaking of us. Through this baptismal anointing we are handed over to Christ; we come to share the life and the mission of Christ himself. We too are sent to fulfil the Father's will and to be light and life for others.

In Confirmation, too, we were anointed with the same chrism. In this sacrament we are strengthened for the public life of discipleship we are entering. Confirmation's gift of the Holy Spirit equips us for the struggle of discipleship, with all the heartache and opposition it can bring. It instils in our innermost being the gift of hope, that supernatural virtue by which the things of this world are seen in their true perspective. Through this gift we know where to place our lasting trust. We learn not to be dismayed when the fortunes of this life turn against us. Rather we remain steadfast in the promises of the Lord and help others to enjoy such life-giving hope.

So the call of Christ, which has summoned this young man to ordination, has also called each of us to a particular path of discipleship. Each of us is marked out. Each of us has received the gift of the Holy Spirit needed for our calling.

The demands of this discipleship, the claims of God, lie on us all. What are they?

Day by day we are to live a life of prayer. Not a day should go by when we do not raise our hands in prayer. Only in prayer do our hearts truly express themselves. Only in prayer does our anointed inner self find its true focus and self-expression. God has made us his own. When we turn to him, then, we find our true selves, just as instinctively as a flower turns to the sun and opens its petals.

Then, through our holy anointing, we seek to live in a manner which fits our new dignity as sons and daughters of our heavenly Father. A life of self-control, restraint and reverence for others is a hallmark of those anointed with chrism. It is important to remember that this includes, crucially, the chastity of behaviour fitted to the calling of each of us. Today that is a particularly vital witness, one much needed in our society.

We will also be a people who are constantly seeking and giving forgiveness. The hallmark of our heavenly Father is his desire to call us back to himself, to repair the damage done. So too for us. Through the anointing we have received, we are placed on the road of reconciliation, always seeking to mend, repair, restore the good work of him in whose name we now act.

All who are anointed into a new bond in Christ will also be men and women of compassion, offering care not scorn to those in need. And we will be a people who accept the daily struggle for fidelity. We know we will not succeed, and that we will need the compassion of others in our weakness. Yet we will never lose sight of the seal of our anointing, that mark of God's ownership. We will never be rejected by him who gave it. He is always faithful to the anointing he has given. We strive, always, to do our best to live up to it.

The anointing of baptism and confirmation have the same source as the anointing of this ordination. Jesus, the Christ, the Messiah, is the one source of anointing. His titles tell us he is 'the anointed one' for that is the meaning both of the Greek word 'Christ' and the Hebrew word 'Messiah'. Each of the anointings we receive is an effective expression of Christ's choice to draw us into himself, to share with us his mission, given to him by the eternal Father.

These anointings also highlight all that this mission entails. Among the people of Israel this was well understood. The prophets were anointed for their task of setting before the people the easily forgotten demands of the Law and the constant message of God. The priests were anointed so that, in the name of the people, they could make atonement for sin and recall the saving actions of God from the past. The king, too, was anointed, for by his rule he was called to establish order and harmony, reflecting the peace of the promised kingdom. Prophet, priest, king, each had a part to play in guiding, building and sustaining the community.

But one was to come in whom these tasks would come together. His action and his word would be at once prophetic, priestly and regal. He would finally establish the kingdom in himself. In him would be fulfilled the promise of salvation. He is the one of whom the angels sang: 'Today, in the city of David (who was anointed king) is born for you a saviour who is Christ the Lord.' (Luke 2:11) To the name 'Jesus', which means 'saviour', is to be added 'Christ', the anointed one.

Through our anointing we share in these tasks of Jesus the Christ. In our lives we are to speak like a prophet, keeping before all whom we meet the gracious and life-giving Word of God. We are to be priestly, bringing all things to God in prayer, striving to make our world a holy place. And we are to be 'agents of the kingdom', setting patterns of relationships, of honesty, trust, reliability and justice, so that the signs of the kingdom are never lacking.

Today in this ceremony it is the priest who is anointed. By this action he is called to share in the prophetic, priestly and kingly role of Christ as Head of the Church. Not only is the entire Body of Christ called to be 'the anointed one' in the world today, but it is also given this sacrament by which it is to be guided, shaped and governed. Through the anointing of ordination, the priest will work 'with the order of bishops'[1] in the service of the Church. He will act 'in the person of Christ the Head' in all that he does.

In this ceremony it is the hands of the priest which are anointed. From this day on, these hands will be raised in prayer and entreaty at the altar, on behalf of the people. These hands will be held out in invocation of the Holy Spirit so that our offerings of bread and wine may become the Body and Blood of Christ. These hands will lift before us that same saving presence of Christ. And God will use these hands to impart on us his blessing as the Mass is ended.

In the Sacrament of Reconciliation, the hands of the priest are raised in absolution, bringing the cleansing of our sins and the restoration of peace in our hearts. These hands will anoint the sick and the dying.

In all these gestures, the hands of the priest act for Christ. It is as if the priest has given his hands to Christ for him to use as his own. Just as in baptism we are entrusted by the Father into the hands of Christ, so too Christ uses the anointed hands of the priest so that he can tend us and fulfil the tasks given to him by the Father.

For these reasons there has long been a custom of not only receiving the first blessing of a newly ordained priest, but also of kissing his hands. The oil of chrism is still fresh on those hands. Christ has just made them his own. Over the years ahead they will be used in all the outward signs of the hidden grace of the sacraments. They will, of course, also be used for all the normal tasks of life. They will move tables and stack chairs; they will cook and help with the washing up; they will pull out lottery tickets and hand over winnings. The hands of a priest will be shaken by so many, so often, at times of sorrow and in moments of celebration. They will wave greetings across the street and knock on countless doors. They will flit across the computer keyboard, and the TV remote control. No doubt at times, they will be used in actions or gestures which are hurtful and damaging. And the wrongdoing will reverberate all the more strongly because they are the hands of a priest.

But on the day of ordination the hands of the new priest are, for us all, a lovely focus of the promises of God, a symbol of the anointed one, Christ himself, who is always in our midst. These hands, too, are a focus of our joy and of our thankfulness to God, the giver of such good gifts.

Today, as we seek the gift of the Holy Spirit to create a new priest, so too we ask the Lord to renew in each of us the effectiveness of our own anointing. May the power of the Holy Spirit fill our hearts again today. May that Spirit refresh in us the effects of our baptism, enfolding us in the embrace of Christ and emboldening us to be Christian in word and deed. May this Holy Spirit confirm in us the courage to be witnesses to hope in a world that seems to be closing in on itself. May we always point to the horizon of God's promise, the promise of lasting peace for all who love him. And we pray for our new priest that he will be a faithful minister to all to whom he is sent, being for them the instrument of God's forgiveness, compassion and love.

Notes

[1] *Rite of Ordination to the Priesthood,* (see p146)

Missioners

A Prayer of St Francis

You are Holy the only God.
you do wonders
You are Strong, Great, the most High.
You are the almighty King.
You, Holy Father, the King of
Heaven and Earth.

You are Three and One.
You are good, all good,
the highest good.
Lord God, living and true.

You are love, chastity.
You are wisdom, humility, patience.
You are beauty, meekness, security.
You are inner peace; joy; our hope.
You are justice, moderation, all our riches.
You are enough for us.

You are beauty and meekness.
You are our protector,
our guardian and defender.
You are strength and refreshment.

You are our hope, our faith, our charity.
You are all our sweetness.
You are our eternal life.
Great and wonderful Lord.
God Almighty, Merciful Saviour.

Amen.

Let us begin to serve the Lord

*Based on the homily given at the Ordination to the Diaconate of
Brother Michael Pooley, St Edmund of Abingdon and
St Frideswide, Oxford, 1 July 2006*

Every candidate for ordination to the priesthood is already a deacon. And he will always remain a deacon.

The diaconate is an essential part of the Sacrament of Holy Order. It is not wiped out by the other steps of that one Holy Order: priesthood and episcopacy. When a deacon is ordained a priest, and a priest ordained a bishop, they do not lose the character of the diaconate. Rather the diaconate gives the fundamental shape to all that the priest and bishop do. The diaconate is all about service. Being a priest or a bishop is about service too.

The deacon is the servant of Christ and of the people. He serves in the name of Christ. Indeed a good understanding of the service offered by the deacon is that of an ambassador. He acts and speaks in the name of the one who sent him. He makes his master present. In particular, his task is described as one of 'waiting at tables'. In other words, he brings from the storehouse of his master all that is needed for the wellbeing of the Lord's people. He brings to the people the effective service of charity, the practical organising of the

Church's service of those in need. He brings the Word of God from which that charity springs and he plays his part in the Liturgy of the Church which is the celebration and renewal of that life-giving love.

The dalmatic worn by the deacon remains, figuratively at least, the vestment of every priest and every bishop, imprinting on all his actions this underlying quality of willing service. Indeed one of the common aspects to be found in the ordination ceremonies of deacons, priests and bishops is the prostration of the candidates before the Lord. This gesture of self-abandonment is the prelude to the accepting of the commission, the gift of the Holy Order.

It is worth remembering that St Francis of Assisi was a deacon. He was not a priest. Somehow the position of deacon fitted his profound spirituality of poverty best of all. He knew that the best way of appreciating the gifts of God is to be free of one's own possessions, one's own security, and to live fully dependent on the goodness of God.

In fact Francis was so intently aware of the loving God, who bestows every good gift, that he spent his entire life attempting to respond to the generosity of Lord. He knew he could not achieve all that he longed for. But he knew that his best hope lay in this abandonment to God. As he died he returned to this same point. In his last hours he asked to be taken from his bed and put onto the bare floor. He wanted to lie prostrate before the Lord again. He said these words:

Let us begin to serve the Lord

'Let us begin, brothers, to serve the Lord our God for up to now we have made little progress.' (St Francis)

Today each of us can repeat these same words, renewing within ourselves the love that inspires us. We pray especially for all deacons and priests that they, too, will be renewed in their desire to serve the Lord in a spirit of detachment, simplicity and joy.

Indeed, Francis is well known as 'God's troubadour' for the many ways in which he proclaimed the goodness of God and our need for repentance. His entire yet short life was a song of praise to God. The joy that God gave him came shining through the hardship he endured and the intense and continual pain of the stigmata of his last years. In this, too, he fulfilled his diaconate and is a model for all deacons.

At the centre of ordination ceremonies there is a handing over of key objects, or 'instruments'. They symbolise what lies at the heart of the ministry that is being received. The priest is handed a paten and a chalice containing the bread and wine for use at Mass. The deacon is handed the book of the Gospels, in a gesture accompanied with these words:

'Receive the Gospel of Christ whose herald you now are. Believe what you read. Teach what you believe and practice what you teach.' [1]

This is the deacon's mandate. And it remains the mandate of the priest, too. Francis lived this mandate in exemplary fashion. He did not hesitate to use his imagination in expressing the events of the Gospel. We owe to him the lovely and enduring practice of creating the Christmas crib to express visually the wonder of the Incarnation. Francis set up the first crib in Greccio in 1223.

Francis, the poet, expressed the Gospel constantly in prayer and praise. He was enthralled by the contrast between the wonder and majesty of the Almighty God and the poverty and wretchedness of our own world. Nowhere was this contrast more sharply expressed, and God's gracious love more clearly seen, than in the mystery of Christ's presence in the Eucharist: the simple substances of bread and wine containing the entire riches of the Godhead.

Even beyond this, God did not hesitate to use the body of Francis as an additional and dramatic way of expressing the invitation to every person to unite themselves totally with Christ. Towards the end of his life Francis' hands, feet and side carried and showed the wounds of Christ himself, wounds from which our salvation flows and which are the ultimate gift of a loving Father. This was, surely, the utter fulfilment of Francis' diaconate. Now, in his entire person, he was a herald of the Gospel.

Ordination to the diaconate and to the priesthood gives the gift to accompany the handing over of these 'instruments'. Through ordination, the particular gift of the Holy Spirit is given to deacon and priest. If each is faithful the gift enables him to fulfil his calling. The Holy Spirit alone can heal and raise our hearts and inspire our minds so that we, too, can use our imaginations, our well-chosen words and our bodily life and actions for the proclamation of the Gospel.

Part of me would like to make a small and prosaic addition to the handing over of the Gospel book to a new deacon. I would like to give him a clock and a notebook as well! Time and reflection are essential for anyone who is to proclaim the Gospel, and to do so in the name of the Church. The clock would stand as a reminder of the need to make time each day for prayer and pondering. The business of life, whether in the parish or at home, easily swallows up all our waking hours. But everyone who is to preach needs to set aside time for preparation and prayer. Without it our efforts will be facile.

So, too, the notebook is important. It is a sign of the need for personal reflection, that steadiness of gaze on the experience of life, on the events of a day. This gaze seeks to see all that happens in the light of the Gospel. In this kind of reflection we seek out the shadow of sin in all that we have done or said, as well as the brightness of the presence of the Holy Spirit who brought cheer to us, even in unexpected ways and moments. This kind of reflection reads the Gospel into our own experience, and our own experience into the Gospel. It allows us to permit the Holy Spirit to illustrate and correct our living, and helps us to see how life in Christ brings its daily concrete demands.

Time and reflection are crucial in the development of the preaching of priest and deacon. They help to transform initial general thoughts into something that is focused and related to a particular time and place. They help to bring the Gospel down to earth, here and now. They also help to bring out of a broad Gospel vision a specific leadership for a set of circumstances. Time and reflection change idealism and general exhortation into a call for a particular service; they change goodwill into focused and effective action. Without time spent in prayerful reflection our overall fervour will be lost and we will be left with a rather empty shell, of fine outward appearance, but little within of the constant, particular demands of living each day by the Holy Spirit alone.

For this reason we do well to remember that living the Gospel always takes place within the community of faith, within the Church. Everyone who seeks to journey on this path needs the encouragement, and correction, of a wider community. Together we engage in the challenge of working out what the Gospel requires of us in each and every circumstance. Only within this wider context can we avoid the temptation of reducing the Gospel to affirmation of our own insights and the challenge of the Gospel as being directed only towards others.

Indeed we need to remember the axiom of St Augustine that we have no scriptures, no Gospel, unless the Church give them to us. This is why our prayer, reflection and study of the biblical message is always to take place within the Church and shaped by its teaching. The Gospel entrusted to deacon and priest is handed over by the bishop. The Church entrusts this Word to its ministers. The Word is to be used, broken open, in the name of the Church, too.

In the ordination of a priest, the new priest receives the paten and the chalice with the bread and wine they hold. These are the 'instruments' of his office as priest. They are for the sacrifice he is to offer. Through it he invites the people to union with Christ in the inner bond of grace.

These gifts are, of course, the work of human hands. They represent our daily living with all its efforts and toil. These gifts, like all work, gain their meaning from the love that lay behind their making. The self-giving of the worker, in skill or drudgery, is what gives the fruit of our labour its true value. In this way the gifts brought to the altar are gifts of love. They are the fruit of love in their symbolic meaning too, for they represent the daily effort of family life, of cooperation with colleagues, the joy of life's good moments as well as the bitterness of its failures. All is brought to the altar, to the hands of the priest, to be made one with the sacrifice of Christ.

This takes place only through the power of the Holy Spirit given to the priest through ordination. Only in and through the Church, animated by the Holy Spirit, does this great exchange of gifts take place, for what we place on the altar becomes the Body and Blood of Christ given to us for our nurture and salvation.

This mystery of the Eucharist is the making of the Church. Through the gift of the Holy Spirit and the receiving of Christ, the Church – you and I – is again formed as the Body of Christ in the world. This is the everyday work of the Mass: forming, reforming, reconciling the Church, and all its members, into the Body of Christ. In this way every celebration of Mass reminds us of our deepest identity, of who we truly are. It teaches us that our true existence lies in the life we share in Christ; that this life is for ever; that this identity gives rise to our best actions and most noble aspirations. Every sacrifice of the Mass makes plain to us that we find our true happiness when, in faith, we are ready to live by sacrificial love. Then we know our natural impulse of love has matured and grown into the likeness of Christ, who loved and did not count the cost.

Every ordination ceremony is an example of that love. The gift of priesthood and diaconate is received because the gift of a life has been made. Whenever generous love comes into being, then God can give his remarkable gifts. We pray that the gift of priesthood and diaconate, and the grace which accompanies them, will sustain every priest and deacon with the same level of generous self-giving that fills his heart on ordination day. So too we pray that the grace of marriage will sustain in every couple a continuation and maturing of the love with which they first gave themselves to each other. In their loving they too proclaim this same mystery of Christ.

Even though we speak of the self-giving of deacon, priest or spouse, as something that they do, we also know that this gift is itself prompted by the Holy Spirit. It is never entirely our own work. Quite often we have to admit that we don't quite know where our generosity comes from. It is a gift of God. For this reason it finds its home and its fullest expression within the household of God, the Church. That which is given by the Holy Spirit rightly pertains to the life of Christ and rightly enriches the Church, his Body.

So we say that priesthood and diaconate are always given in and by the Church. This is true both of the desire and the gift itself. No one presents himself for priesthood. No one is ordained in his own right or his own name. The gifts are given for the entire body, for service and the building up of love within the Church. So holy orders are exercised always within the body of priests and deacons and in union with the bishop. It is always and entirely for the good of the people. And in being so, it is also for the good of the priest or deacon himself.

Today we pray that the profound exchange of gifts which we witness here will bear great fruit under the power of the Holy Spirit. We pray that the words of the Scriptures will be a true revelation of God, every day of this deacon's life. We pray that the bread and wine given into the hands of the priest each day will, in the sacrifice of the Mass, bind him closer to Christ unto eternal life. We pray that priests and deacons will remain steadfast in this ministry of Holy Order in the Catholic Church.

And we pray for each other, that the Holy Spirit will renew in us that joyous service which is such an unmistakable hallmark of his presence.

> *'Let us begin to serve the Lord our God for up to now we have made little or no progress.' (St Francis)*

Amen.

Notes

[1] *Rite of Ordination to the Diaconate (see p158)*

Missioners

From the Gospel of St John

As the Father has loved me,
so I have loved you.
Remain in my love.
If you keep my commandments
you will remain in my love,
just as I have kept my Father's commandments
and remain in his love.
I have told you this
so that my own joy may be in you
and your joy be complete:
love one another,
as I have loved you.
A man can have no greater love
than to lay down his life for his friends.
You are my friends,
if you do what I command you.
I shall not call you servants any more,
because a servant does not know
his master's business;
I call you friends,
because I have made known to you
everything I have learnt from my Father.
You did not choose me.
No, I chose you;
and I commissioned you
to go out and to bear fruit,
fruit that will last;
and then the Father will give you
anything you ask him in my name.
What I command you
is to love one another.

Chapter 15:9-17

Love and Sacrifice

*Based on the homily given at the Ordination to the Priesthood
of Paul Haines, St George's, Worcester, 22 July 2006*

The ceremony of the ordination of a priest is a rich tapestry. It is an interweaving of words, gestures, symbols and images. Each has its own particular significance; each highlights an aspect of the gift of Holy Order and of the life and ministry of the priest. Together they give eloquent testimony to the underlying fact and truth of this moment: here God is at work.

Of course this ceremony has involved a great deal of hard work. Everything has been carefully prepared, an effort in which many people have been involved: servers, choir, those who decorate and care for the church, those who have prepared the liturgy, and those who have made ready the reception taking place after Mass. Each of you has made your own preparation too: what to wear, what time to leave home, and many other things besides.

Yet what we are celebrating here is not the coming together of all that effort, but the work of God. Our work prepares the setting, nothing more. All our activities are preliminary, not of the essence of this occasion. Through these preliminaries we prepare our hearts to receive, from God, this great grace.

The particular gift given today is that of a new priest. But at this moment, and throughout this ceremony, God wishes to enter afresh into the heart and soul of each of us. Here God touches our lives. We have come for this.

As this ceremony unfolds we strive to cooperate in the action of the Lord. Yes, we admire the beauty of the sights and sounds of this ceremony. But in doing so we seek to enter more deeply into their meaning. With the eyes of faith we see beyond the surface of these events to their inner, more hidden, reality. Then the ceremony becomes a moment of grace for us all.

Central to the themes of this ceremony are those of love and sacrifice. They are central here because they lie at the heart of the work of God in our lives. They are of the essence of the life of the priest too.

The experience and reality of love is something with which we are familiar. The experience of loving another, and being loved by another, is one which fills us with such joy. Love gives us inner peace, self- confidence. At times it fills us, again, with a zest for life. Love opens our eyes to all that is good and beautiful, not only in the beloved but beyond, in all around us. Such love is what we desire, what we long for, what we want to have, what we hope we shall never lose.

Sacrifice, on the other hand, seems to be the very opposite. Sacrifice means giving up something of real value. It means precisely doing without something that is desirable and attractive. It means letting go of something that is good in itself and good for me. Sacrifice, in the ultimate meaning of the word, means giving up even life itself, losing that which is most precious of all, and doing so by an act of will.

Yet we also know that despite this apparent paradox, love and sacrifice are intimately linked. In truth, there is no love that does not involve real sacrifice; there is no true sacrifice that is not born out of love. Every married couple knows this; every parent does too; every enduring loving friendship includes this same paradox.

Love and sacrifice are also central to the life of Christ. They are twin themes which make up the mystery of our salvation in the life and death of Christ. Inevitably they characterise the life of the disciple too.

In Christ we see the love of God made visible. In him we see the Father, the One who generates all life, lovingly sharing that gift of life with us. Creation is the outpouring of the Father's love, flowing life into our teeming world. Because this creation is a work of love, then not only does it possess real beauty but it also has within it a clear destiny. The work of the Father's love is not made for oblivion or futility. The work of love is never pointless. Rather, this work is destined for ultimate fulfilment, for all things will, at the last, be filled with the glory of the Father. And Christ is the one in whom and through whom this work of love is both brought about and brought to its completion.

In Christ we also see the gift of the Holy Spirit at work. The Holy Spirit, it can be said, is the constant loving of Father and Son, in a timeless present, which actually makes life flourish. It is the Holy Spirit who raised Jesus from the dead. In like manner, the Holy Spirit raises up dead hearts, refreshes withered love and reinvigorates dried up relationships. And the Holy Spirit is given from the side of Christ, poured out afresh from his crucified body.

Christ himself, quite simply, is the Way, the Truth and the Life of love. He is love's true portrait. He shows the inner patterns of love in our flesh: its beauty and its demands, its goodness and its cost.

In Christ, then, love and sacrifice come together most perfectly, for the action of love is seen most fully in his sacrifice. This is the ultimate and final portrait of love: his total self-giving, even unto death on a cross. Here love and sacrifice become truly one, inseparable in the fullness of truth and beauty.

The crucifix, then, is love's true image. In it love's inner secret is laid bare for our contemplation. So the crucifix becomes the sign by which we live. It is our shared mark of recognition, our guide and inspiration. This image of loving self-sacrifice is the one with which we bless, by its presence, every room in our homes. The crucifix shows us, again and again, that self-sacrifice is the heart of loving, and that it lays bare the mystery of God, the truth of the Incarnation, the action by which we are made whole.

This image of loving sacrifice runs right through this ordination ceremony.

The candidate will prostrate himself on the floor. That is a gesture of profound self-abandonment, a handing over of his entire life to the Lord. It is an action expressive of the love for the Lord which fills his heart and makes him want, really want, to give his life away.

In the litany of the saints we seek the prayers and support of many who have sacrificed their lives for the love of God and love of their fellow human beings. We call on the English and Welsh Martyrs who died for their faith: Bishop John Fisher, Sir Thomas More, Fr Edmund Campion, Nicholas Owen, Richard Gwyn, Ambrose Barlow and Ralph Sherwin. They were all led, like Christ, to the scaffold to die. We call on St Maximillian Kolbe who volunteered to die a most painful death in place of a condemned man, and on St Edith Stein who went to the gas chambers rather than abandon her Jewish origins and people. We ask for their strength so that, with God's help, we shall show in our lives the same spirit of self-sacrifice.

What is required of us all today is the same spirit, the same heroic courageous spirit. It is certainly required of all priests.

Such generosity, such self-sacrifice, comes only from great love. It has no other source. It is impossible without generous love. Sacrifice such as this comes only from close, intimate friendship with Christ, knowing him as friend, as intimate lover, as the one who, in the love he gives, makes our loving response a real possibility.

This is just what the words of the Gospel tell us:

'A man can have no greater love than to lay down his life for his friends. You are my friends if you do what I command you. I call you friends because I have made known to you everything I have learned from my Father.' (John 15:13-15)

A friend is taken into the confidence of the other. Friends share an inner life; they have an openness, one to another, that is both the fruit of love and the continual nurturing of that love. Secrets do not sit well between those who have great love for each other. It may well be true, as it is between Christ and each of us, that not all can be declared at once. But love gives such a basis of trust that the unknown future does not matter. All that does matter, all 'the master's business' (v.15), is being made known in love.

This crucial business, the heart of 'everything I have learned from my Father' (v.15), is the truth that love gives rise to sacrifice. Jesus learns this, in the end, when he overcomes all those heart-rending temptations and finally says: 'Let your will be done, not mine.' (Luke 22:42) At that point he lets go of himself and embraces the master plan, the final revelation of love. He embraces the cross. This is the Father's will.

Yet the Father, who as creator is the first and continual
giver of life, does not wish life to be destroyed. Life is his
gift of love. But now we see that, in order to put this creation
back on its right tracks, a great further act of love is needed.
The Father wants to 'straighten out' our loving.

We often lose sight of love's true shape, its true dynamic.
Constantly, each day, in our thoughts and actions, we distort
love and reduce it to self-satisfaction. Love, in our hands,
becomes selfish. It ceases to be self-giving. This is our sin.
And it is only healed with its own medicine. Love as self-
sacrifice is the remedy for our sins. This victory is
established, triumphant over every temptation, once for all,
again and again. This is our salvation and it is achieved in
Christ.

In the course of this ceremony, the new priest will be
anointed. So, too, Jesus was anointed immediately prior to
his sacrifice of himself. We read of his visit to the house of
Simon when 'a woman came to him with an alabaster jar of
the most expensive ointment and poured it on his head as he
was at table.' (Matthew 26:7) This extraordinary action
rouses great indignation. But Jesus made its meaning clear:
'She did it to prepare me for burial!' (Matthew 26:13) It is
commonly held that this woman was Mary Magdalene,
whose feast we keep on this ordination day.

So, too, our new priest is anointed in order that he can now
offer sacrifice to God, the very same sacrifice of Jesus Christ.
As this anointing takes place, these words are said:

'The Father anointed our Lord Jesus Christ through the power of the Holy Spirit. May Jesus preserve you to sanctify the Christian people and offer sacrifice to God.' [1]

At every Mass, the priest offers the Body and Blood of Jesus as the great sacrifice of love. It is made to the Father, to fulfil his will, his master plan. Through it our loving, our very world itself, may again be put right. Through this sacrifice the true order of things is again made clear, again restored. Thus sin does not have the last word; and selfishness, which so shapes our world, is put in its place.

Then, in the course of the Mass, it is the priest who sacramentally breaks the body of Christ, pours out his blood, so that they become for us our spiritual nourishment. He gives to the faithful all that is needed to effect in our lives the story of true love, even to its fulfilment in heaven.

This work of sacrifice is at the heart of priesthood. Sacrifice is inseparable from priesthood. This is our Catholic faith and here alone is the fullness of the understanding of the priesthood of Christ to be found.

Shortly, in this ceremony, I will ask the candidate if he is willing 'to discharge without fail the office of priesthood'.[2] This is followed immediately by the question: 'Are you resolved to celebrate the mysteries of Christ faithfully?'[3] These mysteries – these saving graces – flow from this one eternal sacrifice of Christ now entrusted to the new priest.

The priest, of course, is not a functionary. His calling is not simply to offer sacrifice. He must also be a sacrifice himself. His way of life flows from the sacrifice he offers for himself and for the people. He will make an offering of his own life, day by day, in loving response to the offering Christ made of his life for our sakes. So do we all. Yet the priest is bound to Christ in a special way, precisely in this action of his self-sacrifice to the Father. The priest gives his hands and his voice to Christ so that they can be used to make present, in every time and place, that one saving offering. In those actions the priest becomes Christ. So, too, in his daily living he strives to be as like to Christ as he can, fashioning a disposition which, in the words of St Paul, is marked by 'charity, selflessness and patience'. (Ephesians 4:1-2)

As every priest knows, this resolve will be tested in many ways. Patience is often tested on a daily basis as demands are made which seem to be entirely unreasonable. So too his selflessness will ebb away at times. He will find himself wanting, above all, to protect and guard himself, his time, his personal 'space'. And, at times, his desire to show constant charity will give way to a cold sense of duty.

These things happen to every priest. These are our constant struggle. In them we are greatly strengthened by our celebration of the Mass, in which we are given again the wonderful vision and reality of love that gives rise to sacrifice. This refreshes us, restoring in us our sense of purpose and our desire to live, above all else, in and for the Lord.

All who strive to follow Christ give and receive this support. All who try to make their daily life an offering to God, no matter what it contains, play their part in the life of the Church. Today, and every day, I ask you all to do this faithfully. This, above all else, will encourage and reaffirm your priests in their ministry.

In a few moments the gifts of bread and wine for the sacrifice of the Mass are brought to the new priest for the first time. It is an action which will be repeated every day in his life. I pray that as this action takes place each day, he will recall the words that first accompanied it. They are words to be used now. They are words that sum up priestly ministry and, if remembered, will keep that ministry fresh in his heart.

'Accept from the holy people of God the gifts to be offered to him. Know what you are doing and imitate the mystery you celebrate: model your life on the mystery of the Lord's cross.'[4]

To that we can only say 'Amen'.

Notes

[1] *Rite of Ordination to the Priesthood (see p147)*

[2] Ibid (see p142)

[3] Ibid (see p143)

[4] Ibid (see p147)

Rite of Ordination to the Priesthood

CALLING OF THE CANDIDATE

Deacon   Let him who is to be ordained priest
please come forward.

Candidate   Present.

PRESENTATION OF THE CANDIDATE

*The Rector of the seminary presents the candidate for
Ordination by publicly testifying to the bishop and the people
of God that he is ready for Ordination.*

Rector   Most Reverend Father, holy mother Church
asks you to ordain this man, our brother,
for service as priest.

Bishop   Do you judge him to be worthy?

Rector   After inquiry among the people of Christ and
upon recommendation of those concerned
with his training, I testify that he has been
found worthy.

ELECTION BY THE BISHOP
AND CONSENT OF THE PEOPLE OF GOD

Bishop We rely on the help of the Lord God and our
Saviour Jesus Christ, and we choose this
man, our brother, for priesthood in the
presbyteral order.

All Thanks be to God.

HOMILY

EXAMINATION OF THE CANDIDATE

*The candidate now stands in front of the bishop who examines
him on his intention to serve the Church as a priest.*

Bishop My son, before you proceed to the order of
the presbyterate, declare before the people
your intention to undertake this priestly
office. Are you resolved, with the help of the
Holy Spirit, to discharge without fail the
office of priesthood in the presbyteral order
as a conscientious fellow worker with the
bishops in caring for the Lord's flock?

Candidate I am.

Bishop   Are you resolved to celebrate the mysteries of Christ faithfully and religiously as the Church has handed them down to us for the glory of God and the sanctification of Christ's people?

Candidate   I am.

Bishop   Are you resolved to exercise the ministry of the word worthily and wisely, preaching the Gospel and explaining the Catholic faith?

Candidate   I am.

Bishop   Are you resolved to consecrate your life to God for the salvation of his people, and to unite yourself more closely every day to Christ the High Priest, who offered himself for us to the Father as a perfect sacrifice?

Candidate   I am, with the help of God.

PROMISE OF OBEDIENCE

The candidate kneels in front of the bishop and places his hands between those of the bishop and makes the promise of obedience.

Bishop   Do you promise respect and obedience to me and my successors?

Candidate	I do.
Bishop	May God who has begun the good work in you bring it to fulfilment.

INVITATION TO PRAYER

All stand

Bishop	My dear people, let us pray, that the all-powerful Father may pour out the gifts of heaven on this servant of his, whom he has chosen to be a priest.
Deacon	Let us kneel.

LITANY OF THE SAINTS

During the Litany the candidate lies prostrate on the floor in a sign of abandonment to God.

LAYING ON OF HANDS

All stand. The candidate goes to the bishop and kneels before him. The bishop lays his hands on the candidate's head, in silence. Together with the Prayer of Consecration this is the central and most important part of the Sacrament of Holy Order. Next all the priests present lay their hands upon the candidate in silence.

PRAYER OF CONSECRATION

The candidate kneels before the bishop.

Bishop

Come to our help, Lord, holy Father, almighty and eternal God; you are the source of every honour and dignity, of all progress and stability. You watch over the growing family of man by your gift of wisdom and your pattern of order. When you had appointed high priests to rule your people, you chose other men next to them in rank and dignity to be with them and to help in their task; and so there grew up the ranks of priests and the offices of Levites, established by sacred rites.

In the desert you extended the spirit of Moses to seventy wise men who helped him to rule the great company of his people. You shared among the sons of Aaron the fullness of their father's power, to provide worthy priests in sufficient number for the increasing rites of sacrifice and worship. With the same loving care you gave companions to your Son's apostles to help in teaching the faith: they preached the Gospel to the whole world.

Rite of Ordination to the Priesthood

Lord,

Grant also to us such fellow workers,

for we are weak and our need is greater.

Almighty Father,

grant to this servant of yours

the dignity of the priesthood.

Renew within him the Spirit of holiness.

As a co-worker with the order of bishops

may he be faithful to the ministry

that he receives from you, Lord God,

and be to others a model of right conduct.

May he be faithful in working with the order of bishops,

so that the words of the Gospel may reach

the ends of the earth,

and the family of nations,

made one in Christ,

may become God's one, holy people.

We ask this through our Lord,

Jesus Christ your Son,

who lives and reigns with you and the Holy Spirit,

one God forever and ever.

All   Amen.

INVESTITURE WITH STOLE AND CHASUBLE

After the prayer of consecration, the bishop, sits, receives the mitre, and the newly ordained stands and is vested in the priestly vestments. First the stole, the symbol of the authority of the priestly ministry, and then the chasuble, the Mass vestment of service to God and his Holy People.

ANOINTING OF HANDS

Next the bishop receives a linen gremial and anoints with chrism the palms of the new priest as he kneels before him.

Bishop   The Father anointed our Lord Jesus Christ through the power of the Holy Spirit. May Jesus preserve you to sanctify the Christian people and to offer sacrifice to God.

PRESENTATION OF THE GIFTS

A chalice filled with wine and a paten with a communion bread are brought to the bishop who hands them to Father N., saying:

Bishop   Accept from the holy people of God the gifts to be offered to him. Know what you are doing, and imitate the mystery you celebrate: model your life on the mystery of the Lord's cross.

KISS OF PEACE

Lastly, the bishop stands and gives the kiss of peace to the new priest. The other priests present also offer the kiss of peace to the new priest as a gesture of welcome to the Presbyterate.

Rite of Ordination to the Diaconate
The Rite of Ordination begins after the Gospel

The candidate is presented to the bishop by one who has had responsibility for his formation.

ORDINATION OF A DEACON

Calling of the Candidate

Deacon   Let N. who is to be ordained deacon please come forward.

Candidate   Present

PRESENTATION OF THE CANDIDATE

Priest   Most Reverend Father, holy mother Church asks you to ordain this man, our brother, for service as deacon.

Bishop   Do you judge him to be worthy?

Priest   After inquiry among the people of Christ and upon recommendation of those concerned with his training, I testify that he has been found worthy.

ELECTION BY THE BISHOP
AND CONSENT OF THE PEOPLE

Bishop   We rely on the help of the Lord God and our
saviour Jesus Christ, and we choose this
man, our brother, for the order of deacons.

All   Thanks be to God.

HOMILY

COMMITMENT TO CELIBACY

*Required of all deacons except those permanent deacons who
are already married.*

Bishop   By your own free choice you seek to enter
the order of deacons.   You shall exercise
this ministry in the celibate state for
celibacy is both a sign and a motive of
pastoral charity, and a special source of
spiritual fruitfulness in the world. By living
in this state with total dedication, moved by
a sincere love for Christ the Lord, you are
consecrated to him in a new and special
way. By this consecration you will adhere

more easily to Christ with an undivided heart; you will be more freely at the service of God and mankind, and you will be more untrammelled in the ministry of Christian conversion and rebirth. By your life and character you will give witness to your brothers and sisters in faith that God must be loved above all else, and that it is he whom you serve in others.

Therefore, I ask you:

In the presence of God and the Church, are you resolved, as a sign of your interior dedication to Christ, to remain celibate for the sake of the kingdom and in lifelong service to God and mankind?

Candidate   I am.

Bishop   May the Lord help you to persevere in this commitment.

Candidate   Amen.

EXAMINATION OF THE CANDIDATE

The candidate is asked about his intentions to serve the Church as a deacon.

Bishop   My son, before you are ordained a deacon, you must declare before the people your intention to undertake this office.

Are you willing to be ordained for the Church's ministry by the laying on of hands and the gift of the Holy Spirit?

Candidate   I am.

Bishop   Are you resolved to discharge the office of deacon with humility and love in order to assist the bishop and the priests and to serve the people of Christ?

Candidate   I am.

Bishop   Are you resolved to hold the mystery of the faith with a clear conscience, as the Apostle urges, and to proclaim this faith in word and action as it is taught by the Gospel and the Church's tradition?

Candidate I am.

Bishop Are you resolved to maintain and deepen a spirit of prayer appropriate to your way of life and, in keeping with what is required of you, to celebrate faithfully the liturgy of the hours for the Church and for the whole world?

Candidate I am.

Bishop Are you resolved to shape your way of life always according to   the example of Christ, whose body and blood you will give to the people?

Candidate I am, with the help of God.

PROMISE OF OBEDIENCE

The candidate kneels before the bishop and, placing his hands between those of the bishop, makes a promise of lifelong obedience.

Bishop Do you promise respect and obedience to my and my successors?

Candidate   I do.

Bishop   May God who has begun the good work in you bring it to fulfilment.

INVITATION TO PRAYER

Bishop   My dear people, let us pray that the all-powerful Father will pour out his blessing on this servant of his, whom he receives into the holy order of deacons.

Deacon   Let us kneel.

LITANY OF THE SAINTS

During the Litany the candidate lies prostrate on the floor in a sign of abandonment to God.

Bishop   Lord God,
hear our petitions
and give your help to this act of
our ministry.
We judge this man worthy
to serve as deacon
and we ask you to bless him
and make him holy.
Grant this through Christ our Lord.

All   Amen.

Deacon   Let us stand.

LAYING ON OF HANDS

The candidate kneels in front of the bishop who solemnly imposes his hands on the head of the candidate. This is a gesture of invocation of the Holy Spirit. Together with the Prayer of Consecration it forms the heart of the ceremony of Ordination.

PRAYER OF CONSECRATION

Bishop

Almighty God,

be present with us by your power.

You are the source of all honour,

you assign to each his rank,

you give to each his ministry.

You remain unchanged,

but you watch over all creation and make it new

through your Son, Jesus Christ, our Lord:

he is your Word, your power, and your wisdom.

You foresee all things in your eternal providence

and make due provision for every age.

You make the Church, Christ's body,

grow to its full stature as a new and greater temple.

You enrich it with every kind of grace

and perfect it with a diversity of members

to serve the whole body in a wonderful pattern of unity.

You established a threefold ministry of worship and service

for the glory of your name.

As ministers of your tabernacle you chose the sons of Levi

and gave them your blessing as their everlasting inheritance.

In the first days of your Church

under the inspiration of the Holy Spirit

the apostles of your Son appointed seven men of good repute

to assist them in the daily ministry,

so that they themselves might be more free for prayer and preaching.

By prayer and the laying on of hands

the apostles entrusted to those chosen men the ministry of serving at tables.

Lord,

look with favour on this servant of yours,

whom we now dedicate to the office of deacon,

to minister at your holy altar.

Lord,

send forth upon him the Holy Spirit,

that he may be strengthened

by the gift of your sevenfold grace

to carry out faithfully the work of the ministry.

May he excel in every virtue:

in love that is sincere,

in concern for the sick and the poor,

in unassuming authority,

in self-discipline,

and in holiness of life.

May his conduct exemplify your commandments

and lead your people to imitate his purity of life.

May he remain strong and steadfast in Christ,

giving to the world the witness of a pure conscience.

May he in this life imitate your Son,

who came, not to be served but to serve,

and one day reign with him in heaven.

We ask this through our Lord Jesus Christ, your Son,

who lives and reigns with you and the Holy Spirit,

one God, for ever and ever.

All   Amen.

INVESTITURE WITH STOLE AND DALMATIC

The new deacon receives his vestments, outward symbols of his office.

PRESENTATION OF THE BOOK OF THE GOSPELS

The new deacon kneels before the bishop.

Bishop   Receive the Gospel of Christ, whose herald you now are. Believe what you read, teach what you believe, and practice what you teach.

KISS OF PEACE

Bishop   Peace be with you.

Deacon   And also with you.

The new deacon is then greeted, with a sign of peace, by all deacons present at the ceremony.

Bibliography

Champ, Judith, *William Bernard Ullathorne,*
Gracewing, 2006

Garry O'Connor, *Universal Father,*
A Life of Pope John Paul II Bloomsbury, 2005

The Divine Office, Collins, 2002

International Committee on English in the Liturgy,
Ordination of Deacons, Priests and Bishops, Washington
DC, 1975